Why Rape Culture
Is a Dangerous Myth

From Steubenville to Ched Evans

Luke Gittos

SOCIETAS
essays in political
& cultural criticism

imprint-academic.com

Published in the UK by
Imprint Academic, PO Box 200, Exeter EX5 5YX, UK

Distributed in the USA by
Ingram Book Company,
One Ingram Blvd., La Vergne, TN 37086, USA

ISBN 9781845408374

A CIP catalogue record for this book is available from the
British Library and US Library of Congress

Contents

Acknowledgments

This book is the result of conversations with too many people to mention here. I feel very grateful for growing up among people who think seriously about the world. Thanks to all of you.

To everyone at the Institute of Ideas, especially those involved in the Debating Matters competition, the ideal training ground for young thinkers. To Claire Fox, a true political and intellectual inspiration, who has been consistently patient and generous with her time. I learnt a long time ago to listen when she speaks. The same can be said of Helen Reece, whose thinking on this topic I am always trying to catch up with.

To everyone who reviewed early drafts, too many to list here but thank you very much. To everyone at *Spiked*. To Tim Black and Brendan O'Neill for providing invaluable intellectual input. To Rob Lyons, a patient editor who knocked everything into shape, notwithstanding my efforts to knock it out of shape again. To all at Hughmans for teaching me the law.

To my family, who disagree with almost everything I write but who are great fun. I love you all dearly.

And to Nina, who puts up with a lot for the sake of genuine intimacy.

Introduction

On the 13 July 2015, M pleaded guilty to rape. We have to call him 'M' because he is a sixteen-year-old child and is accordingly entitled to anonymity. M suffers from clinical depression and has an IQ of sixty-one, which puts him in the lowest 0.5 percent of the population. He pleaded guilty to raping another boy, who is now fourteen. The victim in the case was the little brother of M's friend. It was alleged that M had forced the victim, over a number of years, to engage in mutual masturbation and oral sex. He had also attempted anal sex.

When the complainant was asked why he hadn't reported their previous activity, he responded that he was scared that his brother would find out and 'call him gay'. The boy's account seemed to portray a complex interaction, which some around the case referred to as 'experimentation'. He never said that M had used violence or physical force. It wasn't the complainant that went to the police. Rather, the complainant told his 'girlfriend', who then told the boy's family[1]. When he was interviewed, the complainant told the police that he felt 'pressured' into doing what M wanted and did not feel as though he could turn him down As a result of his plea, M will be placed on the sex offenders' register and may serve a term of compulsory detention. He will also have a rape conviction on his record for the rest of his life.

---

[1]   While the young complainant referred to the girl as his girlfriend, she herself referred to the two of them as 'friends'.

Of course, we could just call this another successful rape prosecution and be done with it. But when I heard about this case, I had to ask one question: why had we not heard about this case in the media? A clinically depressed child with an educationally sub-normal IQ being prosecuted for non-violent sexual offending against another child two years his junior. Here were two vulnerable children, who had engaged in what some around the case described as 'youthful sexual experimentation', and who were both being dragged into the criminal courts to live their experiments out in public, for the judgement of the adults around them. For all we know, the interactions between the two boys were the actions of two boys confused about their sexuality who felt like they had no avenue to express their uncertainty other than with one another. Did we have no way of dealing with this case which avoided prosecuting? Was slapping the label 'rape' on it the only way we could understand what had happened between these two boys?

It seemed bizarre to me that no one was angry about this prosecution. To my mind, this case was an outrage. No society should treat its most vulnerable in this way. Why had this appalling case, this outrageous miscarriage of justice, not come to the attention of the public?

To answer that question, consider the panicked news stories that do appear around rape. In June 2015, as this book was being completed, the Metropolitan Police in London released a report by a former Scottish lord advocate, Dame Elish Angiolini, into their own handling of rape cases.[2] The report claimed that rape allegations had been 'soaring' in recent years, to the extent that the Met were 'struggling to cope with the number of people alleging they had been raped'. While the number of allegations had increased by sixty-eight percent, there were only seventeen percent more cases prosecuted. The report

---

[2]   *Report of the Independent Review into The Investigation and Prosecution of Rape in London,* Dame Elish Angiolini DBE QC http://goo.gl/l9bv8z

warned that, if current trends continued, the number of 'unpunished rapes' would continue to rise. The report went on to recommend that the law enshrine a statutory definition of when someone was too drunk to consent to sex. Sir Bernard Hogan-Howe, the commissioner of the Metropolitan Police, suggested that rape investigations should be assigned the same level of police resources as investigations into domestic terrorism.

Contrary to the reaction of London's most senior police officer, these figures did not, in and of themselves, provide any basis for panic. The report does not, as some newspapers reported,[3] claim that *rapes* had increased, merely that the number of *allegations* had increased. There are a number of different ways to interpret this increase. It could mean that more and more people are being raped year after year, it could be that more people are willing to make allegations than before, or it could mean that more and more people are thinking they have been raped, but are wrong. The number of allegations tells us little or nothing about the trends in the number of rapes that have actually occurred. It would be quite possible for the number of actual rapes to be falling at the same time as the number of allegations was rising.

Nor is it unusual for there to be a significant difference between the number of allegations and the number of cases eventually prosecuted. In fact, for most criminal offences, the number of prosecutions is far lower than the number of allegations made. With respect to some offences against the person, only three percent of allegations result in a prosecution.

The reaction to this report was typical of the hysterical climate that has arisen around rape. This book is a modest attempt to do two things. The first is to question the expansion of law and regulation further and further into the most private areas of our lives, of which the expansion of rape law is just one

---

3   London faces being 'overwhelmed' by soaring number of rape cases, official report warns, London *Evening Standard*, 2 June 2015 http://goo.gl/F7w7AS

part. Second, it is an attempt to dispel the dangerous myth of a 'rape culture', which is an important element of the current panic. The central argument of the book is that these two trends are feeding an atmosphere of panic around rape, which causes significant harm to both victims of rape and defendants in rape cases. It also has implications for the way we live our intimate lives that extend beyond the criminal justice system.

The claims of rape culture

One of the primary arguments of those who believe that we live in a 'rape culture' is that rape is prevalent and under-reported. It is said that, in the UK, 85,000 women are raped every year and that only a tiny proportion of rapists are ever punished. Social psychological research into 'rape myth acceptance' purports to demonstrate that the public does not understand rape nor what is required to obtain legally satisfactory consent. While this research is subject to robust academic challenge[4], the claims of these research projects are routinely cited as fact in the popular media. Crime surveys routinely suggest that women experience rape, but do not see themselves as rape victims, suggesting that they have — to some degree — internalised rape as a normal part of their sex lives.

Rape culture proponents argue that certain cultural phenomena add to the prevalence and acceptance of rape by 'normalising' sexually aggressive behaviour. Across the country, student unions have banned Robin Thicke's pop song 'Blurred Lines' for contributing to the 'rape culture' on the basis that it includes the words 'you're a good girl, you know you want it'. The song has been widely denounced in certain circles as a 'rape anthem'.[5] A growing list of films have been de-

---

[4]   For critical discussion of 'rape myth' research see H. Reece, 'Rape Myths: Is Elite Opinion Right and Popular Opinion Wrong?', *Oxford Journal of Legal Studies* 2013

[5]   Robin Thicke's Blurred Vision: A Critique of a Rape Anthem in Two Parts, *Truthout*, 4 August 2013 http://goo.gl/6y2Jfb

nounced as contributing to a 'rape culture' by portraying women in an apparently degraded or objectified way. The 2013 film *Spring Breakers*, in which a group of American female students become involved in a crime spree while on a spring break, was said to be 'reinforcing' rape culture by objectifying women. While many have argued that contemporary culture is increasingly 'sexualised', to the extent that sexual suggestion is a more common feature of films and music, an increasing number of people argue today that these cultural phenomena feed a trend outside of themselves that actively encourages the viewer and the listener to engage in sexual violence.

Rape culture is also said to be evident in immature, sexist behaviour, on the basis that it creates an environment in which rape and sexual violence is seen as more acceptable. Sports clubs at universities are described as 'encouraging rape culture' for playing childish games—including the rugby club at Durham University, whose members were accused of trivialising rape by playing a game called 'It's not rape if...'. Apparently the aim of the game was to finish the sentence in the funniest way possible. While almost anyone would agree that the game was juvenile, others went further, suggesting that the game actually facilitated an environment that made rape and sexual violence more likely.[6]

The normalisation of sexual violence is said to be evident in the increased use of the word 'rape' in a flippant or uncaring way. One commentator highlighted how a Facebook group called 'well done wind—you've raped my hair' illustrated a growing trend towards using the word rape as a colloquial verb. 'You've been raped' has, apparently, become a common way to describe any kind of violation. Some say that this, too, is a symptom of a society in which the experience of rape has been trivialised.

---

[6] Durham student rugby club played game 'encouraging rape culture', *Telegraph*, 30 October 2013 http://goo.gl/ZHhzPs

Rape culture is also said to be evident in public attitudes towards rape, particularly in the justice system. The prosecutorial authorities in the United Kingdom regularly refer to 'cultural factors' that hinder rape prosecutions.[7] The 2015 Angiolini report into the investigation and prosecution of rape in London was just one example of the authorities referring to 'attitudinal difficulties' with prosecuting rape. It is often argued that the perceived failure of the justice system to cope with rape is another symptom of a 'rape culture' in the UK.

In the US, the rape culture discussion is particularly fevered, especially in relation to college campuses. A number of recent studies purport to demonstrate that 'frat houses', in which large groups of male students live together, 'facilitate a rape culture' by making young men more likely to rape. One study claimed that living in a frat house would increase a young man's propensity to rape by a third. It is said that one in five women will experience rape or sexual assault in the course of their studies on an American campus.[8] A new film, *The Hunting Ground*, is described as an investigation into the rape culture at American universities and has been a commercial success across America. The idea has even reached branches of the US government. In 2015, the White House asserted that we need to combat campus rape by '[changing] a culture of passivity and tolerance in this country, which too often allows this type of violence to persist'.[9]

The US discussion around rape culture was ignited around a case in Steubenville, Ohio, which will be referred to later in the book. The case involved the sexual assault of a sixteen-year-old girl. Following the conviction of the defendants, all of

---

[7]   Nina Burrowes, *Responding to the challenge of rape myths in court. A guide for prosecutors* http://goo.gl/C8GFo8

[8]   Frat brothers rape 300% more. One in 5 women is sexually assaulted on campus. Should we ban frats?, *Guardian*, 24 September 2014 http://goo.gl/vaWhEk

[9]   Valerie Jarrett, A Renewed Call to Action to End Rape and Sexual Assault , White House Blog, 22 January 2014 https://goo.gl/FBK9p8

whom were teenagers at the time of the attack, the US media was criticised for referring to the case as a 'tragic loss', on the basis that the perpetrators had sacrificed their careers as professional football players. The focus by the American media on the loss to the boys rather than the harm to the victim was cited by many as symptomatic of the normalisation of rape under the 'rape culture'. Another commentator described the Steubenville case as 'rape culture's Abu Ghraib moment', as if the secret creeping acceptance of sexual violence had been exposed to the world, in much the same way that the mistreatment of Iraqi prisoners of war was exposed during the scandal at Abu Ghraib.

The argument that we live in a rape culture is that we live in a society that variously condones, accepts, normalises and even facilitates rape through various cultural phenomena. It claims that rape is common, underreported and that when it is reported the justice system is ill-suited to dealing with it. It claims that we, as a society, are similarly uncaring about rape and have been complicit in its denigration throughout society. The argument of this book is that all of these claims are either demonstrably false or based on extremely questionable evidence.

Dissent

The idea that society in both the UK and the US accepts and normalises rape has not been universally accepted. Since the argument was first formulated, in the course of the rape awareness movement in the 1970s, feminism has effectively been split on the question of whether rape is a 'cultural' trend or a specific and egregious act of violence. The debate has also split campaigning groups around rape. In February 2014, the Rape, Abuse and Incest National Network, a charity based in the US, sent a letter to the White House following the government's announcement about its college rape culture programme:

> In the last few years, there has been an unfortunate trend towards blaming 'rape culture' for the extensive problem of

sexual violence on campuses . . . This has led to an inclination
to focus on particular segments of the student population (eg,
athletes), particular aspects of campus culture (eg, the Greek
system), or traits that are common in many millions of law-
abiding Americans (eg, 'masculinity'), rather than on the sub-
population at fault: those who choose to commit rape. This
trend has the paradoxical effect of making it harder to stop
sexual violence, since it removes the focus from the individual
at fault, and seemingly mitigates personal responsibility for his
or her own actions[10].

The letter cited research showing that between three and
seven percent of the adult male population at college either had
committed sexual violence or would do so. In other words, a
small minority of the college population. This hardly points to
a 'culture', but rather to behaviour that is uncommon. Another
study quoted by the letter demonstrated that three percent of
college men are responsible for ninety percent of the rapes. If
this 'rape culture' were present on American campuses, it
seems that ninety-seven percent of men on campus were
almost entirely immune to it.

Others have raised doubts about the accuracy or 'helpful-
ness' of the term 'rape culture'. Professor Joanna Bourke, who
wrote what is arguably the most comprehensive history of rape
in recent decades, described the idea in the following terms:

> By subsuming (the problem of rape) under a broad term like
> 'rape culture', it obscures the identities of both rapist and
> raped. There is also an unfortunate tendency for those who
> argue for a 'rape culture' to link it with masculinity. I seek to
> argue that rapists are not part of a 'culture' but are the inade-
> quate rejects of a culture of masculinity... The idea that West-
> ern society is a 'rape culture' is one of those phrases that are
> churned out by people who like thinking in clichés . . . The
> notion that 'all men are rapists, rape fantasists, or beneficiaries

---

[10]   The open letter is available here: https://goo.gl/YWEMtC

of a rape culture' (the most important category) is simply not true. It is not good politics either.

In the US, a number of feminist thinkers have been attempting to dislodge the claims made by those who believe we live in a 'rape culture'. Thinkers like Christina Hoff Sommers, Cathy Young and Camille Paglia have all been engaged in a war of information for decades against those who believe we live in a rape culture. Their work will be referred to throughout this book. It provides an invaluable resource with which to challenge the misinformation put forward by those who argue for the existence of a rape culture.

However, the argument of this book is that the rejection of the idea of 'rape culture' has to go further than merely showing that its claims are nonsense. The argument of this book is that it is no coincidence that the rape culture panic has arisen at the same time as fervent intervention by the state in our private and intimate lives. This expansion means we are becoming more deferential to external standards when considering how we should live with one another. This is reflected in many spheres of intimate life. In parenting, a barrage of legal regulation and expert guidance purports to provide the right way to bring up a child. Interventionist family courts are active in removing children from families who get it wrong. In personal, social, health and economics (PSHE) lessons in schools, we teach children that there is a right and wrong way to develop interpersonal relationships, and that doing so any other way can be dangerous. The panic around rape culture is an understandable symptom of a society that is becoming less comfortable with the idea of unregulated, unmonitored intimacy. The panic around rape culture accordingly has nothing to do with rape. It has everything to do with how we live privately with one another.

The myth of apologism

The term 'rape apologism' is often used by those who propagate the idea that we live in a rape culture to describe those arguments that take a critical view on how the law on rape is applied. This was evident following the release on parole in October 2014 of Welsh footballer Ched Evans, after serving half of a five-year sentence for rape. In May 2011, the complainant had gone to a hotel room with Evans's friend and fellow player, Clayton McDonald. Evans had arrived later and commenced having sex with the complainant after his friend had finished. At the trial in April 2012, the jury convicted Evans but acquitted his co-defendant, McDonald. The complainant had been intoxicated at the time of the offence. She was, according to the judge as he handed down the sentence, 'in no condition to have sexual intercourse' and told Evans that he 'must have realised that'.[11]

When Evans was released, the debate about whether he should be permitted to return to professional football split the country like few other cases before it. Evans had already received relatively widespread public support from those who thought that the law had been misapplied in his case. Even those who agreed with the verdict argued that the law on rape had become difficult to understand and interpret. One commentator captured the mood of a section of the public well, when she described the following conversation which she had had in her hairdresser's salon:

> 'Sounds to me like she woke up, realised she'd been dogging, felt really embarrassed about herself and called the police', said Hayley, aged 22. The other young women agreed. Hayley told me she had almost been raped herself, when she was 'totally p-----', by her boyfriend's best mate. She had never mentioned the incident because she thought it would make her unpopular with their social group, who would regard her as a prude...my informal jury at the salon concluded 'if you go to a hotel room

---

[11]   Footballer rape trial: Ched Evans jailed five years, Clayton McDonald cleared, BBC News, 20 April 2012. http://goo.gl/4DG8r

with a footballer you're not going to end up playing scrabble are you?'[12]

On the other hand, many argued that allowing Evans to return to professional football would be symptomatic of our rape culture, which minimises and normalises rape and sexual violence. The article quoted above was described as typical of the 'victim blaming' tendencies that pervade a culture that normalises rape. One commentator referred to the critical commentary around the Evans case as a 'foul chorus' of rape apologism, in which victims are blamed for what happens to them and rapists permitted to return to public life as heroes following their release.[13]

The anxiety about genuine conflict over rape means that people are often punished for expressing unorthodox views. The TV presenter Judy Finnigan was forced to apologise when she suggested that the Evans case was a 'less serious' case of rape than many others.[14] Many suggested that this was a classic instance of rape apologism. Radio host Michael Buerk came under similar fire when he suggested that 'no one came off well' from the Evans case, even the complainant who had returned to a footballer's hotel room drunk and engaged in casual sex. Again, his views were dismissed as 'apologism', for which he was later forced to apologise.[15]

The argument around apologism arose recently in the context of an Irish case. In July 2015, a Norwegian man was successfully prosecuted for raping his girlfriend. The complainant had been on medication to help her sleep. The defendant, apparently frustrated by her intolerance of his

---

[12]   Ched Evans: Sorry, but all rapes are not the same, *Telegraph*, 12 November 2014 http://goo.gl/LfRS96

[13]   The anatomy of rape apologism, *Another Angry Woman*, 22 April 2012 https://goo.gl/5PyhpP

[14]   Judy Finnigan apologises 'unreservedly' over controversial Ched Evans rape comments, *Independent*, 14 October 2014 http://goo.gl/5AEEiS

[15]   BBC's Michael Buerk: I was clumsy to criticise Ched Evans rape victim, *Guardian*, 23 October 2012 http://goo.gl/fK6T2o

watching porn in bed next to her, proceeded to penetrate her while she was sleeping. This happened 'at least 10 times' by his own admission. The judge suspended the man's sentence, meaning he served no prison time, on the basis that a prosecution would not have been possible had the man not confessed everything in emails to the complainant.

Commentary around the case suggested that the judge's sentence was a pertinent symbol of our rape culture. I happen to agree that the judge's decision seems outrageous. Those concerned about the case can rest assured that a similar result would not have transpired under UK law.

However, the danger with the commentary around this case was that it took the judge's decision to be symptomatic of wider cultural trends affecting all of Western society. When the *Guardian* covered the story, the paper claimed that the case demonstrated how pervasive 'apologism' was in the Irish criminal justice system. The same argument is made in the UK, when a controversial or apparently lenient decision is made with respect to a rape case. We will see that, while unduly lenient sentences are still passed in rape cases, the average prison sentence for rape in the UK has increased markedly in recent years. It is a characteristic of the myth of 'rape culture' that particular decisions come to represent broader cultural trends, when the evidence suggests that the reality is the opposite of what the rape culture proponents would have us believe.

It is also common for those who believe in a rape culture to rely heavily on personal accounts of those involved in rape cases, as a means of proving the existence of rape culture. Many of the recent texts that argue for the existence of rape culture are replete with stories of people's experiences of the culture they are describing. While such accounts can be illuminating, one argument of this book is that they tend to present an inaccurate picture of wider social trends. This book could have been full of stories which illustrate the expansion and misapplication of the law around rape, much like other books are full of stories of individual experiences of rape culture. M's is just one story which illustrates the trends under discussion in this book. But, rather than recite endless details about people's experiences, this book will try to focus on developments within the systems which deal with rape and the facts which have arisen from these developments.

Because it focuses away from individual experience, I have little doubt that the argument of this book will be dismissed by some as 'rape apologism'. In a sense, it is unavoidable. The terms of the discussion are such that today, you are either on the side of the argument that we live in an all-pervasive 'rape culture' or you are a rape apologist who believes that the presence and risk of rape has been exaggerated. But if we are to debate seriously whether we live in a rape culture, and what the impact of that idea might be, we need to move on from the dismissal of one side of the argument as 'apologism'. I'll say it boldly: no serious commentator in public life explains away, diminishes or apologises for rape. Rape apologism, in the context of serious discussion, does not exist. What does exist is the critical discussion of how rape law is applied and the concurrent debate around whether and how the current framework reflects our contemporary attitudes around intimacy. This is a vital debate, one that this book seeks to encourage.

Debunking the myth of rape culture

As well as ditching the idea of apologism, this book seeks to argue that the claim that we live in a rape culture is having a seriously detrimental effect on our contemporary discussion around intimacy. The real danger of believing the myth of rape culture is that we become less capable of dealing with difficult moments in our intimate lives and the lives of those around us, without recourse to the law. We will see that the panic around rape makes criminals of our most vulnerable, while undermining the objectivity of the justice system in those cases which do require the intervention of the law. If we are to remain capable of dealing with cases like that of 'M', we need a grown-up discussion about intimacy. We need to finally debunk the myth of rape culture.

My starting point (Chapter 1) is a call to end the numbers game which has dominated the rape discussion for decades. Rape statistics purport to demonstrate a level of truth and certainty which is highly misleading. All the common statistics which present a problematic picture of rape in the justice system are open to multiple interpretations, often to the point that they communicate very little of objective substance. The current debate around rape has become fixated on statistics to such an extent that it is having a detrimental impact on both complainants and defendants in actual rape cases.

Chapter 2 describes how the law has expanded in many areas of our intimate lives. Understanding how rape law functions today requires an understanding that it has expanded alongside many other laws and regulations relating to the most private areas of our lives. The barrage of external influence on our intimate decision-making presents a challenge to intimate judgement, in which relying on one's own interpretation of events in our intimate lives is often called into question. This challenge to intimate judgement is evident both in the discussion around rape and in many other areas of our contemporary discussion around intimacy.

Chapter 3 explains how, far from 'minimising' or 'condoning' rape and sexual violence, the law has expanded significantly around rape towards the regulation of sexual etiquette. Again, many commentators have been dismissed as apologists for pointing out that rape law now targets behaviour that, in the past, would have been considered part and parcel of intimate life. But this change has been reflected in the cases that have set the parameters of the new law. While it has, today, been passively accepted as 'the way the law is', at the time that the legal changes were made they came under heavy criticism for being overly draconian and creating the possibility of serious miscarriages of justice. Law that has become accepted today was deeply controversial when it was passed.

Chapter 4 moves away from dispelling the myths of rape culture, to consider the impact of the panic around rape. The panic around rape problematises the risk and anxiety which is a natural part of intimate life. It presents sex as a process to be managed and controlled to avoid all possibility of risk. The creation of such a distrusting and fearful narrative around intimacy could be fatal to our ability to live and judge our intimate lives without external guidance and management. Further, the belief in rape culture has been used to justify significant limits on freedom in ways that have little to do with preventing actual incidents of rape. It does this by encouraging a degraded and distrustful view of other people and what we are capable of when it comes to negotiating our intimate lives for ourselves.

The book closes by arguing that the belief in rape culture is fundamentally changing society's approach to even the most serious rape allegations. Chapter 5 argues that the panic around rape has given rise to a new form of justice, which prioritises the confirmation and validation of individual experience over and above the objective establishment of the truth. This new form of justice, which is reflective of the distorting panic around rape, threatens the established ways of dealing with all manner of rape cases, to the detriment of complainants and defendants alike.

Conclusion

This book is not about rape. It is not about the hideous criminal offence that takes place every day, and is the subject of arrests, court cases and prison sentences up and down the country. It's not about those rapes that go unreported, those rapes that can ruin lives and render people scared to do all sorts of things they might otherwise have done. It's not about the history of rape in Western societies. It's not about what the law around rape says about the position of women specifically. There are many great books out there about rape, particularly on the history of rape. This book is not about how women suffered rape for hundreds of years without the law taking any notice, nor how the law on rape reflected women's diminished position in society. Those books have already been written by people far better qualified. Their scholarship is referenced throughout.

Most controversially, this book is not focused primarily on the victims of rape. Again, they are mentioned throughout, but only as those who have most to lose from the climate I am describing. The book is not replete with 'survivor stories' — a phrase with which I have a lot of difficulty, given that it suggests that rape inherently carries the possibility of some kind of internal 'death' — and does not dwell on the details of particular rape allegations. Rape victims can suffer in ways I will never have to imagine, and although this book does not centre on those experiences, it does not seek to undermine their experiences.

This book is about the contemporary panic around 'rape culture' that, as we will see, often bears little resemblance to the reality of rape. The argument of the book is that intimate life is suffering under the panic around rape and rape culture. This panic has arisen in the context of a society which is less sure of the parameters of intimate life than ever before. As old narratives of intimate life die away, what has replaced them is not a new, individualised sense of what intimate life is, but a ream of laws, regulations, guidance and expertise about how we should conduct the most private aspects of our lives. This presents a serious challenge to the status of individual judgement about intimacy and, accordingly, the future of intimate life in general.

One

Rape Statistics
Time to End the Numbers Game

The panic around rape culture thrives on misinformation. No other crime is scrutinised so carefully, yet so inconsistently, for its progress through the criminal justice system. We are constantly told that rape has a 'low conviction rate', yet the *Guardian* reported in 2013 that the conviction rate was in fact at an 'all time high'.[1] We are told that the criminal justice system is improving its response to rape, but that only about seven percent of reported cases end in a conviction. We are told that between 0.6 and two percent of rape complaints are false and that ninety percent of rape perpetrators 'get away with it'.

Statistics are important fuel for the panic around rape culture. It is said that the numbers consistently bear out a picture of a failing justice system. Those who believe we live in a rape culture argue that the police are innately suspicious of rape complainants, to the point that trying to get the police to do anything about a complaint is not worth the time. Even if a case does get to court, the complainant will routinely be disbelieved by juries who hold prejudicial and false beliefs about rape complainants. A whole body of academic research has been devoted to investigating 'rape myths' and their effects on juries, purporting to show that the public is prejudiced in its dealings

---

[1]   Rape conviction rate at an all-time high, *Guardian*, 23 April 2013
       http://goo.gl/mGgA8Q

with rape complainants[2]. Some of these researchers have advocated the abolition of the jury in sex cases in favour of trial by judge alone and have also argued for the professional training of jurors to rid them of their 'outdated' attitudes.

The argument of this chapter is that the picture presented by the statistics is often extremely misleading. There is little room for certainty when it comes to rape statistics. Because they attempt to describe the most private areas of people' lives, they are unlikely to reflect people's actual lived experience. Many of the ideas which persist around rape today attempt to attach certainty to statistics which are inherently open to interpretation. More worryingly, the prosecuting authorities in the UK have become utterly fixated on these fundamentally uncertain numbers. It is no longer unusual to hear the police and the Crown Prosecution Service (CPS) talk about the need to 'drive up' the numbers of people charged or the number of people convicted. This represents a concerning abandonment of objectivity and judgement, two qualities which are vital to ensuring that the law around rape is properly and fairly applied.

Are there really 85,000 rapes a year?

Today in the UK, we are often told that rape is happening on an 'epidemic' scale. Newspapers report that the conviction rate is 'stubbornly low', considering the sheer number of rapes that take place. It is said that rape is significantly underreported and that women believe that rape is 'too trivial' to report, or that they are terrified of engaging with a justice system which they think will ignore them. One commentator wrote in late 2014, following the debate regarding Ched Evans:

> Coming forward in a culture that devalues female experiences
> of violence is extremely difficult ... if we really want to see a

---

[2]   For critical discussion of 'rape myth' research see H. Reece, 'Rape Myths: Is Elite Opinion Right and Popular Opinion Wrong?' *Oxford Journal of Legal Studies* 2013

dramatic shift in how rape is dealt with as a crime we need to change our society's treatment of violence against women. But there are still so many women who are terrified of reporting rape because the institutions that ought to be helping them threaten, traumatise, vilify and ultimately fail them.[3]

This commentary is a typical example of the 'rape culture' narrative. It claims that our culture still fails to take sexual violence seriously, and that this results in women being terrified of reporting because they may be left traumatised by the process of dealing with uncaring institutions. We will see that, while these are common arguments from those who say we live in a rape culture, they are lacking any convincing evidential support. The evidence about the under-reporting of rape is ambiguous and open to different interpretations. Of course, there are women who fail to report in order to avoid engaging with the justice system, but there is no evidence that there are 'many' of them. The evidence we do have suggests that the justice system is better equipped to deal with rape than it ever has been, and has been getting better. In fact, the reforms to make the prosecution of rape easier are now diluting the traditional rights of defendants, on scant evidence that any further reform is required.

The claim that 85,000 women are raped or severely sexually assaulted every year was obtained from the Crime Survey for England and Wales (CSEW). In 2013, the survey stated that '0.5 percent of females report being a victim of the most serious offences of rape or sexual assault by penetration in the previous twelve months, equivalent to around 85,000 victims on average per year', with only fifteen percent of those being reported to the police. The data from the survey was included in a 2013 statistical bulletin, called *An Overview of Sexual Offending in*

---

[3] Jinan Younis, Women are still terrified of reporting rape, *Guardian*, 28 October 2014

England and Wales.[4] The bulletin concluded that while rape is not a common crime, the incident rates for many other offences being far higher,[5] the crime remained significantly 'underreported'.

The 85,000 figure certainly sounds like a lot. That's 235 rapes and serious sexual assaults a day, or nine incidents every hour. If it is true that 85,000 women are raped or seriously sexually assaulted every year, the fact that only around 1,000 people are eventually convicted of rape in a given year looks scandalous.

But a closer look at the CSEW raises questions about whether we should take the figure of 85,000 at face value. Once you consider the methodology of the survey, the 85,000 figure in fact tells us far less than some rape campaigners would have us believe. The CSEW figures are based on a face-to-face survey. According to the survey methodology:

> The questions asked do not use technical terms or legal definitions but are phrased in plain English language. The information collected during the interview is then reviewed later by a team of specialist coders employed by the survey contractors (currently TNS-BMRB) who determine whether or not what was reported amounts to a crime in law and, if so, what offence has been experienced.

This process is known as 'offence coding'. Answers are gathered by trained reporters, and then grouped into instances of particular offences. Of course, the interviewers do not review evidence or obtain any other accounts of the incident in question. In relation to sexual offences, respondents to the survey were asked:

---

4   *An Overview of Sexual Offending in England and Wales*, Ministry of Justice, Home Office and Office for National Statistics, 10 January 2013 https://goo.gl/RVlNIU

5   The CSEW estimated that 2.2 percent of the adult population had been victims of violent offences resulting in injury within the last 12 months, compared to less than one percent having experienced rape.

Which, if any, of these things has someone done to you in the LAST 12 MONTHS, that is, since the first of [DATE] when you made it clear that you did not agree or when you were not capable of consent?

YOU CAN CHOOSE MORE THAN ONE ANSWER AT THIS QUESTION IF YOU WISH

1. Penetrated your vagina or anus with a penis, even if only slightly

2. Penetrated your vagina or anus with an object (including fingers) even if only slightly

3. Penetrated your mouth with a penis even if only slightly

4. ATTEMPTED to penetrate your vagina or anus with a penis, but did not succeed

5. ATTEMPTED to penetrated your vagina or anus with an object (including fingers) but did not succeed

6. ATTEMPTED to penetrate your mouth with a penis but did not succeed

7. None of these

8. Don't know/can't remember [6]

If respondents answered 'yes' and marked 1-3, they were treated as a 'victim' and included in the figure of 85,000. The survey then goes on to ask questions about the perpetrators of these actions.

The first problem with this is that someone who is penetrated without consent is not necessarily a 'victim' of rape or serious sexual assault, even in law. The question fails to take into account an alleged perpetrator's knowledge at the time of the incident. Rape requires that the perpetrator lacked an honest belief in consent. Accordingly, the respondents who

---

[6]   The survey methodology is available here: http://goo.gl/6ccybi

answered 'yes' to (say) question (1) would not be a 'victim' of rape if the perpetrator had a reasonably held honest belief that they were consenting. The survey accommodates this partly by requiring that the complainant 'made clear' they were not consenting. But it does not ask how (or when) they 'made clear' this lack of consent nor whether what they did was sufficient to dislodge any belief in consent that their 'attacker' may have had. Nor does the survey ask whether or not the 'attacker' desisted once the lack of consent was 'made clear' — including such incidents would effectively criminalise many examples of normal sexual foreplay, especially between new partners. But significantly, it fails to capture those circumstances where a complainant may have been incapable of consenting, but the perpetrator did not know they lacked such capacity and honestly and reasonably believed they were consenting.

For example, a couple may start having sex before the woman falls asleep. Because the woman no longer had the capacity for consent, but the penetration was ongoing, this could amount to rape. But whether she was being raped or not would hinge on whether her partner believed she was consenting. For as long as her partner had the reasonably held belief that she was consenting — that is, for as long as he remained oblivious to her falling asleep — this would not amount to rape. He would lack the requisite guilty mind. The question as posed in the CSEW does not allow for these cases to be removed from the total.

I asked the Office of National Statistics, which is responsible for administering the survey, about this. The ONS accepted that the survey counts victims who potentially should not be considered as such. The ONS's written response indicates that:

> As you will be aware, the legal definitions of offences are complex and the general public do not generally understand the sometimes subtle distinctions between, for example theft and robbery or rape and other sexual assault. Thus, rather than ask people whether or not they have been victims of specific offences, the survey tries to operationalise the different legal offences in a series of short questions. In doing so, it is accepted

that we will fail to identify some victims and potentially include others who shouldn't be.

So the figure of 85,000 potentially includes as victims people who shouldn't be. Yet the idea that 85,000 women are raped every year is often cited without qualification. There are also serious issues with citing the figure as an estimate. The government's *Overview of Sexual Offending* document reports the findings of the survey as follows:

> It is estimated that 0.5 percent of females report being a victim of the most serious offences of rape or sexual assault by penetration in the previous 12 months, equivalent to around 85,000 victims on average per year. Among males, less than 0.1 percent (around 12,000) report being a victim of the same types of offences in the previous 12 months[7].

What has been added to the figures in the above interpretation is significant: the word 'victim'. Whilst the survey gives the best possible picture of how many women have experienced penetration in a manner that could be viewed by the law as rape or serious sexual assault, it does not tell us how these 85,000 women viewed their own experiences. It does not tell us whether they themselves thought of what happened to them as a crime or whether they thought of themselves as 'victims'. Of course, whether or not a woman viewed themselves as having been raped is not determinative of whether they have or not, but as things stand the 85,000 figure could include all sorts of perfectly ordinary relationship behaviour.

Many of us would have had experiences with our partners that may meet the legal definition of rape, but which, nonetheless, would never be interpreted by either party as rape. Have you ever commenced sex with your partner while they — and you — were partly asleep? A lot of people have. The fifth edition of the *Diagnostic and Statistical Manual of Mental Disorders*

---

7   Ibid (4) above

(*DSM-V*) recognises 'sexsomnia' as a condition affecting a small portion of the general population which causes people to commence sexual activity in their sleep. Even if you don't suffer from a condition, would it really be sensible to think of everyone who has got a bit frisky in the night as a rapist? Perhaps you and your partner have had sex while you were both too drunk to know what you were doing. If so, your partner may well have formed part of the 0.5 percent of respondents to the survey who reported having experienced rape or serious sexual assault in the past twelve months. The law may recognise these scenarios as rape, but to those involved in these incidents, these could be nothing more than the everyday experience of adult sexual life.

The statistics on why women did not report an incident to the police are revealing. Combined figures for 2007-8, 2009-10 and 2011-12 show that, across the periods surveyed, twenty-eight percent of women told no one about what had happened, fifty-seven percent told someone but not the police and fifteen percent told the police (everyone who told the police also told someone else).

Where a woman had told someone but not the police about what had happened, the survey asked why they had not gone to the police. In 2012, nineteen percent said it was 'a private/family matter and not police business'. Another eleven percent said the incident was 'too trivial or not worth reporting'. In other words, of those who told someone but not the police, thirty percent of those respondents made the decision that it was not worth involving the police in what had happened. In contrast, only eight per cent said they 'did not want to go to court' and a further eleven per cent said they did not want to go through 'further humiliation'. Remember that for the periods described above, twenty-eight percent of women told no one what had happened to them. The survey did not ask these women why they did not tell anyone, but it is at least possible that these women also thought the incident 'too trivial' or that it was a 'private or family matter' and consciously chose not to involve the authorities.

So, of the 85,000 'victims' a year, some are not victims to begin with. Twenty-eight percent of these women told no one about what they had told the survey, which may suggest that the incidents that the survey is reporting as serious crime were in fact too trivial to report. In 2012, of those women who told someone but not the police, only nineteen percent said their concern was with the nature of the justice system or the trial process. On the basis of these numbers, there is no evidence to suggest that 85,000 women are 'victims' of rape or serious sexual assault every year. Calling it an 'estimate' is to ignore how women themselves think about their own experiences. There is certainly no sound basis for suggesting that rape and sexual assault is significantly underreported because of concerns with the justice system. All of the complexity and uncertainty involved in the numbers around rape is routinely bulldozed by the narrative that we live in a 'rape culture'.

It is interesting that previous crime surveys purporting to demonstrate the extent of rape did ask women how they felt about what they were reporting. In 2002, the Home Office published a set of statistics which showed that 'one in every 20 women aged between sixteen and fifty-nine in England and Wales has been raped'. This was in response to a survey which asked whether they had been 'forced to have sex against their will' over the past twelve months. When asked how they felt about what had happened to them, fewer than two-thirds of respondents actually thought of themselves as victims of rape.

Some feminists would argue that this shows how rape has become 'normalised' to the extent that it is not considered a big deal. When American feminist Christina Hoff Sommers criticised the American statistics on campus rape for failing to take account of how a woman interpreted the incident that had happened to her, some feminists responded that this was to suggest that women had become so used to rape that they barely noticed it any more. More recent studies have described the argument that rape is only rape if a woman describes it as such as representing 'stereotypical assumptions many people still hold about rape, considering it to be an act of extreme violence perpetrated by an unknown assailant upon an unsuspecting woman who is willing to defend her sexual purity with her life'[8].

This interpretation places little faith in women. Most women will know when they have been raped. If we are being more generous to women, and trusting their judgement about their own sexual experiences, we could say that what the 85,000 figure illustrates is that in the context of an intimate relationship it is artificial to apply—as these surveys do—a purely legalistic understanding of what constitutes rape to all of our sexual encounters. You are bound to end up with a high figure. In fact, it is surprising that the numbers aren't higher. If you applied the same methodology to assessing the prevalence of battery in England, you would be asking whether respondents had experienced 'unwanted touching' in the past twelve months. Almost everyone would respond positively. Once you remove a person's judgement from assessing a crime, then all sorts of everyday activity will be considered criminal, even if those involved did not experience it as such.

So the picture is more complex than it is often presented. The idea that women are routinely failing to report because they are 'scared' or 'intimidated' by the justice system is not supported in evidence. While a positive response to the survey's questions will render a woman a 'victim' of rape for the purposes of the survey, the survey does not ask respondents whether they viewed themselves as victims. This is victimhood bestowed by bureaucracy. Of course, the figures show that there are still women out there who experience a given incident as rape who wish to make a complaint, but are put off by the prospect of their fears with regards to the justice system. Also of concern is the increase in the number of allegations made to the police over recent years. Whilst it is wrong to describe the increase in allegations to the police as an increase in 'rapes', given that reported allegations do not

---

8   R Warshaw, *I Never Called it Rape*, Harper Perennial, 1988

equate to proven allegations, it is worrying that more and more women are making rape allegations to the police while the conviction rate remains static. However, official attempts to 'drive up' the number of people convicted of rape have actually made this situation worse. While increasing the rate of allegations reported as crimes, whilst also increasing the number of these reports which end in a charge, the conviction rate for rape has begun to fall. This suggests that the panic around rape culture, leading to an official fixation on particular statistics, actually makes the prosecutorial authorities worse at doing their job. Before we examine this in detail we need to debunk the myths that abound around false complaints.

Are only two percent of complaints false?

The claim that only two percent of rape allegations are false is widely deployed by rape-awareness campaigners to claim that men routinely get away with rape. An article in 2014 on the *Huffington Post* claimed that 'males are more likely to suffer sexual assault than to be falsely accused of it' and claimed that false allegations made up 'between two and eight percent' of the total.[9] The statistic is often used to rebut the 'myth' that 'women cry rape'. Of course, this statistic has significant implications for rape cases. If juries know, once they sit down to deliberate, that only two percent of allegations are false, then some may think that there is a ninety-eight percent chance that the complainant is telling the truth. This is hardly starting a trial on a level playing field.

The problem is that the two percent figure, or the eight percent figure, or any other figure claimed is, essentially, plucked out of the air. There is, in fact, no reliable evidence whatsoever for the number of UK false allegations. This is

---

[9]   Tyler Kingkade, Males are more likely to suffer sexual assault than to be falsely accused of it, *Huffington Post*, 12 August 2014
        http://goo.gl/BC0wWX

hardly surprising when the line between what is true, false, unproven and proven in rape cases is often a very fine one indeed.

What is remarkable about the prevalence of the two percent statistic is where it has come from. If you follow the citations for the two percent statistic, they each eventually lead back to Susan Brownmiller's 1975 anti-rape book, *Against Our Will*. This book reports the statistic as being cited in a speech given by a judge in the United States in 1973. There is no citation for the figure in Brownmiller's book. There is no evidence that the judge was relying on anything other than his hunch. Yet this figure is often deployed about the UK, today, as if it has something serious to say about the prevalence of false allegations.

Another figure is sometimes circulated to the effect that 0.6 percent of rape allegations are false. This is also unverifiable. The original figure was published by the Crown Prosecution Service. This, in the UK, has been another statistic used to 'disprove' the idea that women often 'cry rape'.

This figure is even more misleading than the two percent figure and refers only to those allegations which have been proven to be false, and prosecuted as false complaints. To cite this figure as the number of false allegations is simply wrong. It does not take into account those cases found to be untrue by a jury, or those that are discontinued through a lack of evidence. In fact, it is extremely rare for a rape allegation to become subject to criminal proceedings for being false; accordingly, very few allegations that are false will ever be proven false in a court.

In fact, these figures are inherently harmful, as well as being extremely dubious. The focus on 'false' allegations does harm to both sides of a rape case. Citing figures about 'false' allegations creates expectations about the truth of all allegations before they have been tested. If it is 'rare' for a complainant to 'make up' what has happened to them, then immediately it becomes more likely that they are telling the truth. The truth is that the number of 'false allegations' is unknown, and could never be known. 'False' is not the same as unproven and unproven is not the same as false. The very status of 'true' and 'false' in rape cases is a difficult category. An allegation does not necessarily 'become' true because it ends with a conviction, notwithstanding the fact that we as a society respect the verdict of a jury. At the same time, an acquittal does not necessarily mean an allegation is false. Only two people know the truth of what happened with respect to a particular allegation, and even then uncertainties abound. There are no reliable figures for the number of false allegations in rape cases. There never will be.

The recording rate: failing victims?

The official fixation on statistics is making the prosecutorial authorities worse at prosecuting allegations of rape. The recording rate refers to the number of allegations reported to the police that get recorded as crimes. In 2011, this figure came under scrutiny when it was revealed that there was a vast disparity between the recording of sexual offences in different police areas. In Gloucestershire, only two percent of allegations made to the police were 'no crimed', which meant that two percent of allegations were recorded as not disclosing a criminal offence—for example, if a neighbour reported a woman being 'raped', but on further investigation it transpired that no crime had taken place. In Kent, thirty percent of rape complaints made to the police were ended with a report of 'no crime'. This led to widespread suspicion that the police were 'routinely' no-criming reports as an alternative to investigating them.

These findings led to a report by Her Majesty's Inspectorate of Constabulary (HMIC) in January 2014, which was damning with respect to its findings on police reporting. It found that 'of the 3,246 decisions to cancel, or no-crime, a crime record that we reviewed, 664 were incorrect. These included over 200 rapes and more than 250 crimes of violence against the person'.[10] These were based on reports between November 2012 and October 2013.

The police responded to the negative press by 'criming' more offences and referring more cases to the CPS. In October 2014, the Office for National Statistics released figures showing that twenty-nine percent more rapes had been recorded as crimes since the findings of the HMIC report. The increase in reporting was widely reported as a victory for the police, with the ONS commenting that the increase was partly due to improvements in crime recording. The CPS, too, sought to push more cases through to a prosecution. The *Violence Against Women and Girls Performance Report* for the year 2013-14 concluded that while the police 'crimed' seventeen percent more reports during 2013 - 2014 and the CPS charged twenty-five percent more cases, the proportion of convictions dropped for the first time in six years to 60.3 percent. This pattern was repeated in 2014-2015, when the figures showed an increase in both recorded rapes and charges, but a further fall in the conviction rate to 56.9 percent, its lowest since 2007-08. While the police have been recording more allegations as crimes, and CPS lawyers were charging more cases, they were failing to build cases sufficiently strong to get a conviction. In other words, they were prosecuting more weak cases.

So the obsession on behalf of the police and prosecutors with regards to statistics has arguably made them worse at prosecuting. The drive to increase the number of allegations ending in a charge and a conviction actually leads to a greater number of unsuccessful prosecutions. It also demonstrates a worrying abandonment of objectivity with respect to these cases. The decision whether or not to charge a case should not be taken on the basis that doing so will increase performance

---

[10]   *Crime-recording: making the victim count*, HM Inspectorate of Constabulary, November 2014 https://goo.gl/y1dnCU

statistics. It should involve an objective and impartial judgement on the evidence.

Perhaps inevitably, the CPS has blamed lingering 'rape myths' for the falling conviction rate. Alison Saunders, the current director of public prosecutions, said:

> Even though there have been slightly more defendants convicted, the steady increase in conviction rates we have seen in recent years has halted, and this must be addressed immediately.[11]

But this is dangerous nonsense. As we will see, juries are in fact more likely to convict rape complainants than in most other cases that come before them. Saunders is also ignoring history. In the 1990s, the police pledged to charge more rape cases, and the conviction rate dropped then, too. The pattern suggests that when the police and CPS seek to charge more cases in order to 'improve' their figures, the conviction rate drops. Charging a defendant with an offence and then failing to get a conviction indicates that prosecutors have let down both the defendant and the complainant.

This problem is arguably being exacerbated by recent prosecution policy. Both the police and the CPS have encouraged their staff to 'believe' rape complainants are telling the truth from the start. The chief inspector of constabulary, Tom Winsor, recently told BBC radio that 'the police need to institutionalise a culture of believing the victim. Every time.' But 'belief' is not always a good thing, if your job is to collect and assess evidence impartially. If the police are being told to 'believe' at all costs, doesn't it make sense that they may not bother to investigate as thoroughly as they might once have done? We no longer require corroboration for complainant's evidence in rape cases, which means that a witness statement from a complainant is enough for prosecutors to charge the

---

[11]   CPS and police announce new measures to tackle rape, Crown Prosecution Service, 6 June 2014 http://goo.gl/XfCeNw

alleged assailant. It is at least possible that the combination of relaxed evidential rules and an official willingness to believe complainants is detrimentally effecting the investigation of rape allegations.

This would support the views expressed by the lawyers I spoke to. Prosecuting barristers often bemoaned the number of rape cases coming to court that had not been properly investigated. Opportunities to build a case had been missed, because officers had assumed that a detailed witness statement from the complainant would be enough to ensure a conviction. One prosecuting barrister I spoke to said that rape trials were becoming 'psycho-sexual examinations' of two people's unsupported word. In other words, the need to 'believe' has the perverse effect of heightening those elements of the trial process that rape campaigners of the past sought to limit: the focus on 'proper' sexual behaviour and questions about who was drunk and whether the complainant could have got out of the situation earlier.

The narrow focus on numbers in the debate around rape is harmful. Almost always, statistics are open to multiple interpretations and do not show what the reporting claims they show. In relation to the reporting and charging rates, the misinformation actually encourages poorer performance on behalf of the prosecuting authorities. By charging more cases to 'push the numbers up', both the police and prosecutors are abandoning their duties of impartiality. This harms both the defendant, who gets charged on weak evidence, and the complainant, who is given the false hope of securing a conviction on the same weak evidence.

Conviction rates: A Stern warning

The use—or misuse—of statistics in the public discussion on rape has a long history. None more so than the allegedly static 'conviction rate', which is trotted out routinely to justify any number of dodgy claims about the justice system. In 2010, Baroness Vivien Stern, a peer in the House of Lords, was commissioned to hear evidence from practitioners, academics and criminal justice staff about the manner in which rape cases were reported. Her remit included investigating the popular notion that the conviction rate in rape cases was particularly low.

She found that the claim that rape had a low conviction-rate was almost always based on a misunderstanding of conviction rates. Stern pointed out that it was often said that the conviction rate for rape remained 'stubbornly' at around six percent. This was completely wrong. Stern said this was only true if you calculated the number of convictions for rape in relation to the total number of reports made to the police. This number, which was indeed around six percent, in fact referred to the 'attrition rate' for rape[12]. This was not unusually low compared to other serious offences.[13]

In fact, the term 'conviction rate' usually refers to the number of cases that *reached court* and ended in a conviction[14]. The conviction rate for rape, as traditionally understood, was in fact, at the time that Stern was writing, around fifty-five percent — meaning that fifty-five percent of cases that reached court ended in a conviction. This was higher than for a lot of other offences. According to the CPS's own figures, this rate has continued to rise since, reaching an all-time high of sixty-three percent in 2012-13[15]. This means that, once a case gets to court, it is more likely to end in a conviction than not.

There was also no evidence that juries routinely disbelieve rape complainants. Stern noted:

Analysis of all 4,310 jury verdicts for rape from October 2006 to March 2008 across all courts of England and Wales finds that rape does not have one of the lowest conviction rates. With an

---

[12] This figure relates to the number of initial allegations resulting in a conviction

[13] *The Stern Review*, Home Office, 2010 http://goo.gl/U9RvYT

[14] Ibid, page 43

[15] Rape conviction rate at an all-time high, *Guardian*, 23 April 2013 http://goo.gl/mGgA8Q

overall jury conviction rate of 55 percent, juries actually convict more often than they acquit in rape cases.

This meant that for all cases that reached a jury, for all cases in which a jury retired to consider whether or not to convict a defendant, they chose to convict more often than they chose to acquit. This should have come as a shock to those campaigners who had been propagating the idea that complainants in rape cases didn't stand a chance in front of what were claimed to be highly prejudiced and ignorant juries.

Stern also highlighted the negative effects that misreporting the conviction rate was having, by misleading complainants into believing that their case would not stand a chance:

> It is clear to us that the way that the six percent figure has been allowed to dominate the public discourse on rape, without explanation, analysis and context, has been to the detriment of public understanding and other important outcomes for victims.

Stern found that the reforms that had taken place over the previous twenty years had left the justice system in a better position than ever before to deal with rape cases. The vast majority of those giving evidence to Stern's commission, from lawyers to campaigners and members of the police, found that nothing more could be done to boost the number of prosecutions and convictions. The old system, in which misogynistic assumptions and assertions held sway, was gone. There was an implicit recognition in Stern's report that the reforms around rape had changed the system as far as possible to maintain a healthy conviction rate, without interfering too heavily in the objectivity of the trial process.

Ministry of Justice research in 2010 supports the claim that juries are impartial and objective when dealing with rape allegations[16]. The 2010 report, undertaken by Professor Cheryl

---

[16]   *Are Juries Fair?* Thomas and others, MoJ Research Series 1/10

Thomas of University College London, was the most extensive research into jury deliberations around rape which had ever been undertaken. Among its key findings were that juries passed guilty verdicts in the majority of cases they were asked to consider. The research showed that the jury conviction rate, being that rate of cases in which a jury retired to consider a verdict and subsequently returned a guilty verdict was as high as sixty-nine percent in some areas of the country, meaning that jurors were considerably more likely to convict defendants than acquit them. The research also showed no evidence for racial bias against black defendants, even in all-white juries.

Notwithstanding Stern's warning about the over-reliance on statistics in our discussion on rape, we are still panicking about conviction rates. The *CPS and Police Action Plan on Rape*, which was first published in April 2014, was announced to coincide with figures suggesting that the conviction rate for rape had dropped by three percent in the years 2013-14[17]. To put this into context, this drop of three percent followed a six-year consecutive increase in the conviction rate, to an all-time high in 2012-2013. As we saw above, the Action Plan has not improved the conviction rate, which has now fallen to its lowest level since 2008. Rather than rethink their approach to these cases, Alison Saunders, who was responsible for the new action plan, said that the drop in convictions by three percent showed that what was required was 'a renewed challenge against persistent myths and stereotypes [the police and the CPS] believe are still having a negative impact on cases'.[18] However there was no evidence whatsoever that the drop in conviction rate had anything to do with attitudes. Rather, as we have seen, history suggests that when the CPS place them-selves under pressure to charge more and more cases, they

---

[17] The CPS conviction rate refers to the number of rape cases charged which end in a conviction for rape or a lesser offence. This is not the same as the jury conviction rate as described by Thomas and Stern.

[18] CPS and police announce new measures to tackle rape, Crown Prosecution Service, 6 June 2014 http://goo.gl/XfCeNw

simply end up charging cases on weak evidence. The most extensive juror research has shown no evidence for juror bias against complainants. The recent fall in conviction rate is more likely to be a result of the CPS's own policies as it is a result of pervasive 'myths and attitudes'.

The ongoing cycle of misinformation around the rape conviction-rate is unforgivable, given the long history of its misuse. Five years after Stern gave her review, warning against the misuse of the conviction rate, some facts should be stated in plain sight: the latest evidence shows that juries are more likely to convict a rape defendant than acquit him and are more likely to convict in a rape case than for many other offences. The conviction rate for rape, meaning the ratio of cases charged which end in a conviction, is still high, especially considering that it is an offence that often lacks objective corroborative evidence. This has been true for decades. Small drops in the conviction rate are not statistically significant over time, and there is no evidence that a fall in conviction rate is occasioned by the prejudices of a jury. In fact, all the available evidence suggests juries are objective and fair when dealing with rape allegations. All of these facts are routinely denied by those who propagate the myth of rape culture.

Conclusion

It is time to end the fixation on statistics that governs the contemporary debate around rape. There is no reliable evidence for the claim that rape is 'underreported'. The evidence that there is remains open to multiple interpretations. There is no reliable evidence for how many allegations are false. Believing that there is prejudges allegations that must be considered with objectivity and impartiality. No one is helped by the pressure put on the police and CPS to drive up the numbers of charges and convictions. The only result is charging more weak cases, leading to more unsuccessful prosecutions.

If the rape-culture proponents are genuinely concerned about victims, then they should stop circulating the kind of information that will discourage complainants from seeking justice. The facts that we do have allow us to give a reasonably optimistic picture to rape complainants. Of course, police practices can be improved and incompetence will always be a risk. Of course, going to court is difficult and sometimes traumatic. But rape is not a numbers game. It functions in a world in which the gap between truth and falsity is often finely drawn. Pretending there are certain inalienable truths about the state of rape in the justice system is misleading, and does significantly more harm than good.

Two

The Real Roots of Rape Culture

The State's Colonisation of Intimacy

We have seen how the current debate around rape functions in an unhelpful climate of misinformation. The argument of the next two chapters is that, contrary to the myth of 'rape culture' — which tends to claim that the law ignores or minimises rape and sexual violence — the law has expanded significantly over recent years into the most private areas of our lives. The panic around rape culture is a symptom of a society in which private, unregulated intimacy has become viewed solely as a site of potential risk. While navigating the risks inherent in intimate interactions was once part and parcel of what it meant to be free person, today the impulse to live out our intimate lives outside the reach of the state is commonly portrayed as potentially damaging. The panic around rape culture is one aspect of this trend.

Over the course of the twentieth century, it seems clear that we have shed many of the social and political pressures that forced us to live our intimate lives in a particular way. Recent discussions in academic sociology have described how the invention of reliable contraception, the greater freedom of women and the liberalisation of marriage have all contributed to a more flexible and personalised notion of what intimacy should look like. The sociologist Anthony Giddens character-ised the state of intimacy in the 1990s as inhabiting a space 'free from the bonds of reproduction' and 'moulded to the traits of personality'. In other words, sex and intimacy can mean what we want them to mean.[1]

There is, of course, much to be optimistic about regarding the freeing of our intimate lives. When, in the 1960s, feminists argued that the 'personal was the political', they were drawing attention to the stifling, subjugating world that the family home could create. Friedrich Engels, writing in 1884, argued that the bourgeois family turned women into 'instruments of production' serving merely to provide the necessaries for man's engagement in public life. Novels of the nineteenth century portray a world in which intimate life, particularly for women, is stifled by social obligation. The novel form itself arises from this tension between the suffocating pressure of social life and the yearning for individual freedom. The modern world, in comparison with the world at the beginning of the twentieth century, appears to be a world of unprecedented sexual liberation.

However, there is cause for reflection on this optimistic conclusion. These accounts of a 'new intimacy' tend to ignore one key fact: that the loosening of old social and biological restraints around intimate life has resulted in greater state intervention in the most private areas of our lives. In both the UK and the USA there has been rapid lawmaking in recent years to allow the state better access to our intimate relationships. These now extend all the way from how to bring up kids to how we sleep with our partners. This framework of bureaucratic management around intimacy appears to have developed almost concurrently with the apparent freeing up of intimate life from the social and cultural pressures of the past.

This deference to external standards has even been taken up by a new generation of feminists, who campaign vigorously for greater state regulation of our intimate lives. Whereas feminists of the past campaigned for the freeing up of intimate life in favour of individual morality and judgement, many contempo-

---

[1]   A. Giddens, *The Transformation of Intimacy*, 1993.

rary feminists have become vociferous mouthpieces for the
state's model of intimacy and the most vocal champions of the
myth of 'rape culture'. It is those who believe in a 'rape culture'
who argue for the greater 'tightening up' of the laws around
rape in order to increase the number of people who are
prosecuted.

Much like the religious and social orders of the past, questioning the new state-sanctioned model of intimacy is often
attacked as heresy. Questioning whether rape law has been
applied too broadly is dismissed as apologism. Arguing that
both men and women should be responsible for negotiating
their intimate lives is dismissed as victim blaming. Arguing
that there should be an assumption that the home should be a
relatively law-free zone, where people should be free, as much
as possible, to live out their lives in the absence of external
interference, is seen as a justification for domestic violence and
emotional abuse.

The paradox of the panic around rape culture, which suggests that the state is not doing enough to control our intimate
relationships, is that it survives today notwithstanding the fact
that the state is more involved in our intimate lives than ever
before. While the law on rape is an important aspect of the
state's management of intimate life, it is just one aspect. Before
we examine how the expansion of rape law allows for minute
regulation of sexual etiquette, we should explore how the law
has become more involved in managing the most private areas
of our lives.

Regulating intimacy

The discussion and debate around the regulation of intimacy is
already raging among academics, especially in the United
States. Some have argued that the freeing up of old social
relations, particularly in relation to women, requires the law to
emerge into a 'new legal paradigm', which acknowledges the

new freedom accorded to people to negotiate intimate lives for themselves[2]. Many have acknowledged that the relationship between the state and our intimate lives has been forced to change with the onset of modernity. Some have argued that the old distinction between a private sphere, an area in which the law was established to protect us from external interference as far as possible, and the public sphere, in which people acted in accordance with wide-ranging and shared standards, has now effectively broken down. The personal has become the political. The argument of this book is that this opening up of private relationships to more direct legal intervention has become a threat to genuine intimacy. The regulation of private relationships that has arisen in the UK has become overly 'welfarist' in character. Welfarist legal reform has been characterized by Jean Cohen as 'regulatory, interventionist, and direct'[3]. It seeks to protect the legal subject by enforcing goal-orientated legislation and practice. In the context of the regulation of intimacy, this involves the law taking a more managerial and interventionist role in private relationships. Recent reforms, of which the reforms around rape law form a relatively small part, have provided the state with the means to manage people's private relationships, especially those which come to be seen as 'problematic', to a far greater extent than has ever been the case before. These reforms have been overtly political, and have played into a narrative which presents intimate life as fundamentally a site of risk in need of management. It is this view of intimate life, one which sees unregulated interaction merely as a site of potential harm, which dominates official and public discussion of intimacy today.

The regulation of intimacy takes place across a variety of apparently disparate areas of law. Accordingly, the interference of the state in our intimate relationships takes a number of different forms. Lawyers will argue, with some justification,

---

2   Jean L Cohen, *Regulating Intimacy,* Princeton University Press 2002

3   Ibid

that a number of different legal trends govern the development of the law in the areas I am about to discuss. This is arguably why the developments in rape law have not been considered alongside the development of the law into other areas of intimate life in the past. Accordingly, the following section is likely to raise issues for legal scholars, who will no doubt be able to identify a number of legislative and common law changes that allowed for the current system of law to ascend to the statute book.

However, the argument of this chapter is that all of the legal developments discussed in this section and in the chapter that follows represent an important trend which occurs—to some extent— outside of the law. The fact that the law and external regulation are able to manage our intimate relationships to a greater extent today than ever before speaks to a weakening of the idea that certain areas of life should be—to as great an extent as possible—shut off from the normal rules which govern public life. Today, the increased involvement of the law in managing our intimate relationships speaks to a depletion of the private sphere to the extent that even our most intimate judgements about how we live with one another become open to official challenge. We see this evident in the panic around rape, but also in many other areas of contemporary life. Firstly, we will consider the state's regulation of intimate relationships in the sphere of domestic violence. We will then consider recent interventions by the state in two of the central institutions of intimacy, namely the family and marriage. We will then consider how these new laws present a challenge to the status of our own judgements in our intimate lives, a challenge which is reflected in the panic around rape and rape culture.

Domestic violence to emotional abuse

Few documents demonstrate how risk-focused the state has become in its regulation of intimacy than its recent policy documents around domestic abuse. The last government's policy around the family was informed by its 2010 policy paper, *A Call to End Violence Against Women and Girls*. The paper emphasised how 'elimination' of domestic violence was to be a guiding 'vision' of coalition policy. The home secretary, Theresa May, consistently emphasised the importance of 'early intervention' in family life to prevent the 'risk' of violence from arising. 'Violence against women and girls' (VAWG) has today become a collective term for crimes taking place in an intimate setting. The Crown Prosecution Service now treats VAWG as a 'performance management category', meaning the CPS publishes annual statistics around its performance in relation to VAWG and the figures around charges and convictions are scrutinised in a manner similar to the statistics around rape.

The government's stated aim of 'eliminating' VAWG has been used to justify new and wide-ranging legal interventions into people's intimate relationships. This has included introducing new offences targeting what once would have been considered perfectly ordinary intimate behaviour. Many of these new offences are considered under the umbrella of VAWG and are included in official performance statistics. We will see how this means that the category can also be used to over-inflate the risks inherent in intimate relationships, by collating together statistics around very disparate groups of criminal offences.

The first measure that was introduced following the 2010 policy paper was the Home Office's Domestic Violence Disclosure Scheme, implemented in 2015 and popularly known as Clare's Law. The law was named after Clare Wood, who was tragically murdered at the hands of her ex-partner, George Appleton, in 2009. Wood was unaware that Appleton had a history of violence against women. The scheme allowed for any member of the public to make an application to the police for information about a person's previous convictions. If the police took the view that a conviction against the particular person was relevant it could be disclosed, in order to assist that person or the person to whom the information was intended to help to make a decision about staying in the relationship.

Despite the fact that Clare's Law was one of the founding policies emanating from *A Call to End Violence Against Women and Girls*, it was met with almost unified opprobrium, especially from those who campaign around domestic violence policy reform. Refuge, a charity providing refuges to battered women, said the scheme would be 'ineffective' unless it provided women to whom disclosures were made with a 'route out' of their relationship. Providing a woman with information about her partner would do little other than destabilise what might otherwise be a stable situation. Other charities pointed out that the scheme could bring unwanted attention on vulnerable families, particularly as disclosure could be applied for by third parties, who had nothing to do with the family other than their suspicion.

Clare's Law, the first major scheme to emanate from the government's 'vision' of eradicating domestic violence, showed the authorities' disregard for the importance of intimate information. In the course of the Clare's Law pilot and consultation — in which the scheme was given a decidedly mixed reception — the value of privacy was a background issue. There was no consideration of the potentially destabilising impact that the availability of such information could have. When the police reported back on the scheme, they referred to it as a 'success' based solely on the fact that over 1,000 disclosures had been made. They had no information about the impact of the disclosures, nor any information about whether the outcome of the disclosures had been positive or negative.

This casual approach to the regulation of intimacy has been reflected in the development of the criminal law. In 2015, the word 'intimate' hit the statute books for the first time. The Serious Crime Act criminalised 'controlling or coercive behaviour' within an 'intimate' relationship. Such control or coercion would not have to be physical; in fact any 'controlling or coercive' behaviour would be potentially covered if it had a 'serious effect on the victim' of that behaviour. The examples given included 'controlling your partner's finances' and controlling where and when they are permitted to socialise.

The criminalisation of 'controlling or coercive' behaviour shows that the law is blind to the reality of relationships. Some

degree of 'coercion and control' is fundamental to any function-
ing relationship. It is hardly unusual for power dynamics in a
private setting to be influential and even determinative of how
people behave. Anyone who claims that they have never
controlled or coerced their partners, even in a way which has a
'serious' effect on them, is likely to be lying. It would be hard to
coordinate meal times or balance family budgets if you didn't
have some degree of control over your partner's behaviour.
Becoming someone's partner necessarily involves giving up a
degree of autonomy for mutual benefit. But the passage of the
law was widely ignored by the commentariat, who tended to
see the move as a legitimate measure to combat the risk of
domestic violence.

This is largely because it is assumed, across the board, that
the law will only apply to certain kinds of relationships. Only
certain people will have their private lives routinely interrupt-
ed by the police, social services or the local council under these
new laws. When I asked lawyers I knew whether they thought
such a law was a problem, the answer was always the same:
the police and the prosecutors would not, I was told, intervene
in those cases where it is not truly necessary. This assumption
captured the essence of the problem: that these new laws,
captured under the new and vague category of VAWG, gave
significant power to the state to decide the legitimate parameters of intimate life.

This is not the only new criminal offence that grants new
powers to the state to regulate our intimate behaviour. In 2010,
the coalition government criminalised 'stalking' for the first
time. The definition of stalking was not included in the statute,
but academic opinion at the time the law was passed suggested
that stalking could include: 'desiring a mixture of reconciliation
and revenge…as a result of a relationship dissolution'; '[pursu-
ing] an intimate relationship with an individual perceived as
their true love, but [when] their attentions are not wanted'; and,
perhaps most worryingly, 'intellectually limited and socially
incompetent individuals desiring intimacy… [but who] lack
sufficient skills in courting rituals'.

For many, the definitions of 'stalking' offered above describe fairly normal behaviour in a relationship. Anyone who has been in love is likely to have gone at least some way to behaving in a manner which could be defined as stalking. In fact, desiring revenge and reconciliation, declaring unrequited love and incessantly pursuing the object of your desire have been considered perfectly normal elements of human relationships for centuries. Of course, stalking can be a genuine problem. Cases can involve deeply troubling obsessive behaviour that can become extremely difficult to cope with. But the law as drafted is drawn so widely that many perfectly normal aspects of intimate behaviour could be caught. Today, the kind of behaviour that has been accepted throughout history as part and parcel of intimate life could now land you in a prison cell with a maximum sentence of five years.

There was a proliferation of new domestic violence laws over the term of the 2010-15 coalition government. Domestic Violence Prevention Orders (DVPOs) were introduced in 2013. They allowed the police to apply to a magistrates' court for an order that can allow defendants to be excluded from their family home, prevented from seeing their children and any other restrictions and measures that the police think would be proportional to prevent the threat of domestic violence. The orders can even be made without the defendant having any chance to respond to the police's evidence. Anti-Social Behaviour Orders (ASBOs), introduced under the New Labour government, were similarly used to intervene in situations where domestic violence was perceived as a risk, even if no actual criminal offence has been committed.

The collection of new laws around VAWG have allowed the state to present our intimate lives as inherently dangerous. In 2015, the media reported that a 'record number of people had been prosecuted for offences categorised as violence against women and girls' between 2014 and 2015. The statistics came from the 2015 CPS report into VAWG. That report indicated that 68,601 defendants were convicted for 'domestic abuse', a rise of just under eighteen percent from the previous year. The report indicated that the conviction rate for domestic abuse, being the proportion of cases that reach court and end in a conviction, had remained steady despite the significant increase in prosecutions and convictions overall.

What was absurd about the reporting of these figures was that the number of 'domestic abuse' convictions included convictions for offences that the government had itself only recently created. Convictions for both 'stalking' and 'controlling and coercive behaviour' were included in the domestic abuse figures, which were bound to significantly increase the number of prosecutions given how broad these new offences are. Looking at the underlying data, the volume of convictions for these offences has continued to rise as more and more types of behaviour have been included under the heading 'domestic abuse'. The category of VAWG includes so many disparate offences that the fact that more people are prosecuted for offences under that heading tells us nothing about the dangers inherent in the home.

Of course, domestic violence is a serious problem, but it would be wrong to assume that these new laws take us any closer to 'eradicating' it. Violence in the home is a deeply complex social problem, one that arises in an enormous variety of circumstances. Today, the term 'domestic abuse' has expanded significantly, to encompass all manner of non-violent intimate behaviour. Many of the people involved in domestic violence, especially those who work directly with the women involved, recognise that the law is too blunt an instrument to resolve the complex issues which arise in the intimate setting. These new laws allow for significant state involvement in the most intimate areas of our lives, yet do little to respond to the substantive problem of domestic violence.

Further, seeking to control each and every situation in which domestic violence could arise would require the micromanagement of individual relationships to such an extent that intimacy would cease to have all meaning. Couples who appear 'normal' can one day erupt into violence. So-called 'troubled' couples, who manipulate and control one another emotionally, are not always the ones who fall into patterns of violence. The idea of these laws is that by the state's intervention, people's relationships can be managed such that even the risk of violence is eradicated. This is not only highly draconian but it is also a myth.

The institutions of intimacy

The two key institutions of intimacy, marriage and the family, have become the subject of extensive official interference in recent decades. Of course, some of these changes have been positive and progressive. The liberalisation of divorce laws in the 1960s and '70s meant that people were no longer trapped in loveless or harmful marriages merely because they could not demonstrate one of the established and restrictive grounds for divorce. This generation is the first to have grown up in a society that has utterly normalised divorce. In fact, keeping a marriage together 'for the sake of the kids' is today seen as a form of abuse. The family, too, has undergone significant changes in recent years, leading to a society which is far more accepting of non-traditional family arrangements.

However, we do not have to be precious about the decline of 'traditional marriage' or the evolution of the family in order to raise concerns about the casual interference by the state in historically significant institutions of intimacy. Recent decades have seen the state become far more active in its interference with both the family and traditional marriage. These interventions have indicated a disregard and animosity on behalf of the state towards the traditions of intimacy, an outlook that is arguably reflected in its wider willingness to interfere in other areas of our intimate lives.

The family is the site of official interference like never before. Recent studies from the University of Kent[4] demonstrate how the proliferation of guidance, regulation and law around

---

[4]   Ellie Lee, Jennie Bristow, Charlotte Faircloth and Jan Macvarish, *Parenting Culture Studies*, 2015.

bringing up kids has led to the emergence of a distinct practice of 'parenting'. Parenting today is often considered to be a specific, pre-defined process that can be subjected to expert management. Every decision made by parents, from whether a mother chooses to breastfeed to how they play with their kids, is now subject to some pre-ordained 'proper' way of doing things. The presence of guidance and expertise in the sphere of parenting shows how family life has been increasingly colonised by officialdom, and the judgement of parents based on their own experience is seen as of secondary worth to the state-approved advice of 'experts'.

In the sphere of law, the family courts have become far more active in their role in managing intimate life. In 2014, the coalition enacted what it called the 'largest family justice reform for a generation', in the form of the Children and Families Act. The act allowed for wide-reaching changes to the way that the family courts operated and included an extendable twenty-six-week limit to care proceedings and limits on the use of expert-witness evidence. The then family justice minister, Simon Hughes, said that the reforms 'focus on the children's needs rather than what parents see as their own rights'.

The review built on a framework of law around the family that often refers to the needs of the child being paramount. But Hughes's remark went further than merely prioritising the needs of the child. Hughes appeared to treat parental rights as something illusory, something that parents 'see', but which aren't there. This troubling remark, to the effect that all parental rights were illusory compared to the will of the state, was glossed over in the popular press, but it hinted at how confident the state had become in attempting to manage intimate life.

The 2014 review reflected an official disregard for parental rights. The central point of the Children and Families Act was to make family justice more 'efficient'. The act followed the independent Family Justice Review[5] undertaken by David Norgrove in 2011, which concluded that the system is often subject to 'unconscionable delay' that was 'fuelled' by a judicial 'distrust of local authorities'. The purpose of legislating was to combat this 'judicial distrust' by making it easier for the courts to order that children be removed from 'problem families'.

The review, with its focus on 'efficiency' and deference to local authorities over the views of parents, showed that the opinions of the family in determining what's best for those involved are held in low esteem by the organs of the state. The family courts hold most of their hearings in secret, meaning that their rulings are not subject to the same level of scrutiny as other courts. Children can be whisked away from their parents in hearings that parents are not entitled to attend. Recent figures from the family court show that the number of children being taken into care has 'soared', suggesting that the court is more willing to intervene in 'problem families' than ever before.[6]

Of course, each of these cases involves significant complexity, but it is hard to ignore the fact that the state has become more willing and able to manage intimate life today than it ever has been before. This is in spite of a number of cases showing how such intervention and management can be harmful. Few cases demonstrated the state's abandonment of familial judgement like that of Ashya King.

Ashya was a four-year-old boy suffering with a potentially fatal brain tumour. In 2014, his parents, Brett and Naghemeh King, removed him from an NHS hospital and fled to Spain seeking proton-beam treatment that had been denied to them on the NHS. The police issued a European Arrest Warrant for the couple, on the basis that they were neglecting their son. A Europe-wide manhunt was mounted for the family, on the

---

[5]   *Family Justice Review: final report*, 2011 https://goo.gl/MgyOI0

[6]   Number of children being put into care soars despite adoption rate freefall, *Independent*, 13 May 2015 http://goo.gl/RNH1hX

basis that they were denying Ashya the treatment he needed to keep him alive. The couple were soon arrested by Spanish police and Ashya was taken immediately into care.

It soon transpired that Ashya's parents had in fact taken all the necessary steps to ensure Ashya was cared for while they were away. They had packed spare batteries for his breathing equipment. They had undertaken all the steps to be able to change his feeding tube while they were not at hospital. But the state authorities had assumed throughout the proceedings that the opposite was the case. They had assumed that Ashya was being subjected to 'wilful neglect' by his parents by daring to defy their ordinances about how he should be cared for. They assumed that the fact that the couple had removed Ashya from the care of the hospital meant that they had been reckless with regard to his care. After throwing the Kings into prison and taking Ashya into care, having made him a ward of court some days earlier, the Kings were eventually released and reunited with their son. The CPS and the NHS authorities eventually conceded that there had been significant failings in the management of Ashya's case.

The state has also taken a cavalier approach to altering contemporary marriage. Of course, the statistics around contemporary marriage suggest that changes are occurring to its value and its meaning that have nothing to do with any interference from the state. Fewer people are marrying than ever before and those that are marrying are doing so later. Child rearing outside of marriage is far from abnormal today. Divorce rates are famously high. All of these arguably indicate that social changes are leading to the meaning of marriage being altered significantly from how it was understood in the middle of the twentieth century.

The changing nature of marriage, and the state's involvement in facilitating that change, became central to the recent debate around the legalisation of gay marriage. For my purposes, what was significant about the debate was the disregard that many of those in favour of gay marriage showed to the possibility that marriage had a particular tradition that was worth defending. Many commentators argued that the argument that marriage had 'tradition' was a complete red herring, some claiming it to be a disguise for hidden homophobia. In my personal conversations on the topic, I noticed that many people who stood up for gay marriage as a progressive reform were often vitriolic and aggressive about those who held on to the idea that marriage had any tradition worth defending. Marriage, according to some, had never really been 'about' anything at all, and those arguing that it had any meaning beyond a 'celebration of love' were simply on the side of reactionary prejudice. In Ireland, where a proposal to legalise gay marriage was supported by sixty-three percent of voters in a referendum, there was pronounced intolerance during the campaign of those who disagreed with gay marriage. Numerous reports emerged of those intending to vote 'no' receiving death threats and being afraid to express their view on the tradition of marriage publicly.

While debate continues about what exactly the result of the Irish vote reflects, there was at least a recognition that such a significant change to a social institution should be put to the public. In the UK, gay marriage was enacted following a narrow public consultation. There was no public referendum and no evidence that the change was supported by the majority of married people. The possibility that married people had any stake in the institution of marriage was simply brushed aside. The speed at which the changes around gay marriage were introduced suggested that the UK authorities agreed not just with the idea of gay marriage, but also with the commentary around the issue that suggested that marriage's traditional meaning was a 'sham'. The consultation document confidently asserted, as did many ministers involved in the discussion, that the meaning of marriage had 'changed'. That might well be true, but the question remained: changed for whom? While the divorce rate, falling marriage rate and increased rate of childbirth outside of marriage suggest that people no longer consider marriage as a prerequisite for having children, these social changes say nothing about the beliefs of those people who choose to get married about the institution they have entered into. The reality is that these people were effectively told that the meaning of an institution they had entered had 'changed', almost overnight. Whether you think gay marriage is a good thing or not, the fact that the state was able to disregard even the possibility that marriage, one of the key institutions of intimacy, had a tradition that some people may care about is a further example of how confident the state has become in defining and attempting to regulate people's intimate lives. We will see that the state's casual, unthinking interference in marriage provides a precedent for its cavalier approach to regulating sex, in the form of the ever-expanding remit of the law around rape.

Today, the two key institutions of intimacy — marriage and family life — have been the subject of significant official interference and modification. The idea that marriages and family life are best understood by the people involved has become seen as risky and in need of control. The idea that people should be able to marry for 'traditional' reasons is seen as reactionary and prejudiced. The idea that parents should be able to dictate what is best for their children is dismissed as wilfully neglectful or abusive. The decline of these institutions as sacred spaces — free, at least to some degree, from the presence of the same rules and regulations that manage life in the outside world — means that we are less likely to trust our own judgement when it comes to our intimate lives. The unrelenting intrusion of the state into our privacy has given rise to a challenge to intimate judgement, in which even our perceptions of what has happened in the most private areas of our own lives becomes open to question and reinterpretation against the purportedly objective standards imposed from on high.

Was I raped? The challenge to intimate judgement

The intrusion of the law into our private lives has created confusion about how to cope with intimate life. A search on Google for the question 'Was I raped?' gives rise to a litany of checklists, all provided by various charities, setting out the circumstances to check for when assessing whether you have been raped. These all purport to offer clear guidance about what constitutes rape. Ironically, almost all of them get it wrong. They say things like 'any unwanted sexual activity that you experience from another person is a sexual assault, sexual abuse or a rape'. Of course, this is not true. 'Unwanted' is not the same as non-consensual. A person can agree to have sex even if they don't want it for all sorts of reasons. Even if sex in a particular situation were non-consensual, whether you were raped would depend in part on the state of mind of the person you are accusing. These charities present intimate life not as something spontaneous, to be lived and negotiated in the moment, but something to be managed at all costs, like parking a car or landing a plane.

Rather than providing certainty about how to think about intimacy, this further perpetuates uncertainty about intimate life. One study, which is typical of the material used to support the idea of a rape culture, claims to show that rape and other forms of sexual violence are 'normal' for many girls, and that such incidents merely fit unnoticed alongside other events in their sex lives. This, apparently, explains why rape is under-reported. As we have seen, there are serious issues around the claim that rape is underreported. However, the narrative that this study suggests is commonly adopted: that the lines between rape and sex have become difficult for people to define.

This uncertainty about classifying sexual experiences makes it entirely normal for people to 'realise' they have been raped after the fact. In 2014, Lena Dunham, a young American female writer, made headlines when she reported that she had been raped some years previously, as a nineteen-year-old student, by a man in her apartment. Dunham is a writer of a hit TV series, *Girls*, which examines the sexual lives of young women in New York. In Dunham's own story, she had invited her 'attacker' back to the apartment, initially engaged him in sexual activity and had even 'convinced herself that she was consenting' to sex. Nonetheless, when Dunham explained the facts of the story to a friend, that friend 'informed' Dunham that she had been raped. Dunham described this story as a rape despite not giving any indication to the man she was sleeping with that she was not consenting.

Dunham was not torn, in the moment, between her moral conscience and her passion. Such a dichotomy is a familiar trope in stories about intimacy. What Dunham describes is not moral indecision, but rather a correction of her own judgement in light of an external, supposedly objective standard. When she was told about the legal definition of rape, when she was told that the contemporary law can place requirements on those we sleep with to ascertain whether or not we consent to sex, her previous judgement about the scenario was usurped. While it is entirely understandable that people of all ages may come to interpret events in their lives differently over time, the idea that we should hold our sexual experiences to some elusive gold standard encourages people to re-evaluate past encounters with supposedly 'objective' eyes.

It is helpful to compare the decisions of Ashya King's parents on the one hand, and Lena Dunham's *volte face* with regards to her sex life on the other. Of course, these cases are different in any number of ways. But there is one factor which distinguishes them significantly in the context of our discussion around rape and rape culture. Ashya King's case involved an assertion of intimate judgement over and above the bureaucratic authority of the state. It involved an admonition of the state's supposedly objective standards for intimate life in favour of a bold statement of individual morality and judgement. Dunham's case involved the opposite: a wholesale re-evaluation of her intimate life in line with the state's standards.

The challenge to intimate judgement has been evident in recent reports around campus sexual violence. In 2015, the *Guardian* published a report into sexual violence at elite universities[7]. Reading some of the stories in the report, it is clear that some complainants are unflinchingly sure in their interpretation of what happened to them, but others seem far less sure about where the line is between normal, youthful activity and sexual violence. One young woman says a close friend kept trying to kiss her, after they had kissed consensually, and then 'refused to leave all night', despite her asking him to 'several times'. She reported this incident to her teacher as sexual abuse. Another described how she woke up in a stranger's bed after a drunken night out. She knew she went into his bedroom consensually, but then said – with respect to what followed – 'I know, academically, that I was raped'.

The idea of academic rape, that you can be raped even though in the moment you did not experience it as such, is becoming more prevalent, especially among young people. This speaks to a weakening of the capacities of certain young people to assert their own judgement over and above the judgement of officials and the law. The challenge to intimate judgement has even been reflected in technological developments. In 2015, an app was launched which allowed users to input their partner's behavior to receive a definitive answer as to whether or not the other person was consenting to their advances. The prevalence of the historical allegation shows how the challenge to intimate judgement has proliferated beyond the ranks of the young. Following reports of allegations of child sexual abuse regarding TV personality Jimmy Savile, there was a seventy percent increase in historic sexual allegations to police. The investigating police forces apparently 'struggled to cope' with the number of allegations. Operation Yewtree, the investigation into the actions of Savile and other high-profile figures in the 1960s and 1970s, has been driven by the public's reinterpretation of the past in line with the supposedly objective standards that we hold today. This trend towards reinterpreting judge-

---

[7]   Student sexual violence: 'leaving each university to deal with it isn't working', *Guardian*, 26 July 2015 http://goo.gl/WXWCwi

ments in our intimate lives has now extended to reassessing whole periods of recent history through the supposedly fresh eyes of contemporary suspicion. Many contemporary commentators talk about the need to 'put the past on trial' when considering allegations of sexual assault and rape from years gone by. It is often argued that the sexual activity of the past can now be reassessed with hindsight as acts of sexual violence. In discussing this chapter with a friend of mine, he described how his mother had indicated that she had realised that the 'so-called sexual liberation' of the 1960s had actually involved 'high levels of sexual assault and harassment'. The sentiment is not unique. The idea that the intimate realm in the recent past was a haven for sexual abuse is thematic through a number of contemporary commentaries. This uncertainty about how to interpret events in our intimate lives means we are worried about discussing relationships outside of the parameters of official guidance and purported expertise.

Consent classes

The fact that we are more willing to defer to external standards when making judgements about our intimate lives is reflected in the recent inclusion of 'consent classes' in children's PSHE (personal, social, health and economic education) lessons. Teaching children how to 'consent' with one another is a disturbing development. It suggests that what was once an organic and deeply human process, the obtaining of agreement from another human being, can be taught to children much like how they learn a musical instrument. The idea that a process like consent might be improvised and lived in the moment, two characteristics which are surely fundamental to childhood interaction, accordingly become problematised and seen as potentially 'abusive'.

In 2013, the opposition Labour Party tabled an amendment to the Children and Families Bill which would introduce 'consent' as part of the national curriculum. The motion followed a report by the children's commissioner which suggested that access to pornography was creating 'harmful attitudes and behaviours' among young people. The teaching of consent was to form part of lessons about relationships, which would also include teaching kids about 'abuse' and same-sex relationships. The shadow home affairs minister, Stella Creasy, said 'we have to teach them not only about the biology of sex but to respect each other and have healthy relationships'.

The amendment was supported by campaign groups, including the feminist organisation Everyday Sexism, which said that

> many of the young people who contact us are confused and scared about sex they have seen in videos shared online or on mobile phones. Others have reported the far end of the playground being called 'the rape corner' and young people saying 'rape is a compliment really' in classroom discussions. It is time to ensure this most vital of topics is properly covered by the national curriculum.

The deeply worrying argument of Everyday Sexism and those in the government who supported these lessons, was that the best way to make children less anxious about rape and sexual violence was to teach them how to avoid being subject to an allegation themselves.

While the idea of teaching relationships in PSHE lessons failed to take flight in 2013, it was wholeheartedly adopted two years later, following the departure of Michael Gove from the department of education. In March 2015, the Personal Social Health & Economic Education Association produced guidance for teachers teaching consent to Key Stage 3 and 4 pupils. The guidance was produced 'in response' to the coalition government's Home Office action plan, *A Call to End Violence Against Women and Girls*. The guidance sought to provide teachers with the means to teach their students about what constituted a 'healthy relationship', one that accorded with 'British values'. It sought to instruct teachers in how to recognise and challenge 'rape myths' and how to recognise 'legally and ethically' when consent was present.

In the context of the rapid proliferation of law and regulation into all areas of family life, the introduction of consent
classes to teach children how to have a relationship that the
state approves of takes on a significantly sinister tone. What are
these 'British values' that young people's relationships are
supposed to accord to? As many commentators have pointed
out, when the organs of government talk about the existence of
'British values' it usually becomes clear very quickly that they
all have different ideas about what such values entail.

The nation's students were one step ahead of the government in introducing consent classes. In December 2014, the
National Union of Students began a pilot campaign called 'I
Heart Consent'. The campaign included a guide for those
involved on how to run consent workshops at their university.
The manual explains that trigger warnings should be used
before talking about topics that could cause upset. Students are
then invited to write down what they think consent is and
what consent is not. Examples of what consent is include
'comfortable', active and 'freely chosen' — hardly adjectives
which would apply to most regrettable, difficult and ambiguous sexual situations that contemporary students will continue
to find themselves in during their first years away from home.

The proliferation of consent classes shows that the rape
culture panic has allowed for the state to take greater control of
how the next generation will think about sex and relationships.
The proliferation of law and expertise throughout all aspects of
our intimate lives means we are less likely to see intimate life as
something to be discovered, improvised and invented, but
rather something that is subject to strict external standards. It is
this challenge to intimate judgement which forms the background of the current panic around rape culture.

Conclusion

We have seen that almost all of the ideas propagated by those
who believe in rape culture are at best uncertain and at worst
demonstrably wrong. Rape is not nearly as prevalent as some
campaigners, commentators and politicians would have us

believe. In the UK we will see that the justice system has been radically reformed so that prosecuting rape today is easier than ever before. Up and down the country, rape defendants are convicted and sentenced to lengthy terms of imprisonment. There is no evidence that the public are unenlightened about the reality of rape, or that their ignorance is a barrier to the prosecution of rape cases. It is a good sign that many people, both in the UK and the USA, have expressed deep and profound criticisms of the rape culture movement and its unrelenting propagation of misinformation.

But what contemporary critics of the rape-culture argument ignore is that the anxiety it expresses is not confined to feminism. It is, in fact, a symptom of the unrelenting intrusion of the state into our intimate lives. It is a result of the state usurping individual judgement about intimate events. It is not restricted in scope to the endless academic arguments about rape and social psychology. It is not merely an academic buzzword dreamt up in gender studies classes. Nor is it an insidious tactic by cranky feminists to target and incriminate men. In fact, the argument that we live in a rape culture is a symptom of a society whose members have become fundamentally anxious about relying on their own judgements about intimate life. This unease, this reaching for supposedly objective standards by which to measure the most subjective realms of our experience, has been used by the state to justify further regulation of our sex lives. This is an important and often ignored element of the context for the dangerous myth of rape culture.

Three

Rape and the Law

We have seen how the current panic around 'rape culture' arises at a time when the state is more involved in our intimate lives than ever before. The argument of this chapter is that the law around rape has similarly expanded its remit to include more and more kinds of sexual behaviour. Over the past two decades, a significant amount of common law has developed around the right and wrong way to have sex. There are now cases that give guidance on when it's legal to have sex with a drunk person; when it's okay to have sex as a transgendered person; when it is okay to wear or not wear a condom. The reason this law has developed is that nowadays people can face prosecution for a wider range of sexual behaviour.

There are two key differences between the old law and the new law that have made rape easier to prosecute. These changes were introduced under the terms of the Sexual Offences Act 2003. Firstly, the new law creates presumptions in certain circumstances that reverse the burden of proof against the defendant. If the Crown is able to prove certain circumstances then the burden falls on the defendant to prove that the complainant consented. Much of the case law that has built up around rape describes the circumstances in which these presumptions apply.

Secondly, the notion of intention has been removed from rape. Under the old law, the Crown had to prove either that the defendant intended to have non-consensual sex with the complainant or that he was reckless as to whether the defendant was consenting. Today, the Crown has to demonstrate that the defendant lacked a 'reasonable' belief in the complainant's consent.

The significance of this change is the remit of the decision granted to prosecution lawyers. When a person is arrested, the evidence against them is presented to a lawyer at the Crown Prosecution Service to decide whether they should be charged. In today's rape cases, the CPS lawyers have to judge whether a defendant's belief in consent was a 'reasonable' one. If they decide that the defendant's purported belief in consent was 'unreasonable', then they can authorise a charge against that person. In other words, today it falls to the discretion of lawyers at the Crown Prosecution Service to decide whether the steps taken by a defendant were 'reasonable' in the lead-up to sex. Falling foul of this standard of 'reasonable' behaviour can be the difference between being charged with rape and not. While the Sexual Offences Act 2003 has been called an 'enlightened regime[1]' by legal academics, I will argue that the significance of the 'reasonable belief' requirement and the addition of the presumptions has been underestimated. These two legal changes have given the courts and prosecutors significantly more sway in setting the boundaries of legitimate behaviour in our sex lives, and made it far easier to charge a defendant than under the old law.

There is an additional factor that undermines the claim that the prosecuting authorities ignore rape. Today, the police and the Crown Prosecution Service are, in fact, more vocal about their prosecution of rape than ever before. Today, a number of commentators have noted how the CPS has become more 'political' in its use of statistics. We have seen how this has arisen in both the context of rape and the peculiar category of VAWG (violence against women and girls). The CPS will often refer to convictions as 'victories' and to acquittals as defeats.

---

[1]   H. Reece, op cit. See also: J Temkin, "'And Always Keep A-hold of Nurse, For Fear of Finding Something Worse": Challenging Rape Myths in the Courtroom' (2010)

This politicised approach to its role undermines its duty towards objective and impartial administration of justice. This abandonment of objectivity is extremely dangerous in the context of rape, around which the law makes extremely fine distinctions.

While those who claim that we live in a 'rape culture' argue that the justice system ignores rape, prosecuting rape is in fact far easier than it once was. Further, our prosecuting authorities have become far more publicly orientated in their prosecution of rape, to the extent that the Crown Prosecution Service will often amend its own rules in an attempt to prosecute more people. Many more situations can be classed as rape today than could be thirty years ago. Cases can be prosecuted on the evidence of a complainant alone, with no need for corroboration. The idea that prosecutors in the UK do not care about rape is undermined by the fact that during the past decade or so the entire system of law around rape has re-orientated in favour of prosecution.

Intention and reasonable belief

The Sexual Offences Act 2003 is often portrayed as a long overdue 'overhaul' of the law around rape and sexual violence, which had existed for most of the twentieth century. It is true to say that before the new law, the law around sexual offending was disparate and spread across a number of statutes. The need for reform was pressing. In 2000, two Law Commission reports recommended reforms to the legal concept of 'consent'. These reports were undoubtedly significant in the development of the eventual drafting of the law.

However, as well as being the product of a certain moment in legal history, I would argue that the Act also arose in a particular political context: the New Labour government. The Sexual Offences Act did not only codify and modernise the old law. It represented a strong intrusion of the law into our private lives. It also formed part of a broader trend in New Labour criminal justice policy towards making the system more victim centred. These two trends, towards greater criminal regulation of privacy and the reorientation of the justice system around the needs of victims, represent two important and often ignored influences on the development of the law of rape.

By 2003, when the act was introduced, the New Labour government was undertaking a thorough legislative assault on our private lives. In 2002, the government introduced the Regulation of Investigatory Powers Act (RIPA), which granted extensive new powers of surveillance. RIPA was New Labour's 'snoopers' charter', and allowed for any public body — including local authorities and even state schools — to undertake intrusive surveillance of almost anybody. The Crime and Disorder Bill, introduced within a year of Labour taking office, led to the establishment of anti-social behaviour orders (ASBOs), which allowed for criminal punishments to be meted out on the basis of causing 'harassment, alarm and distress' to others. ASBOs became the primary mechanism for dealing with domestic incidents within so-called 'troubled families'.

New Labour's most invasive intrusion into family life, one which had significant connotations for the remit of rape law, was its overhaul of the youth justice system, which allowed many more children and young people to be prosecuted for sexual offences. The government abolished the presumption that children between the ages of ten and thirteen were incapable of criminal responsibility, meaning that many more young children could be prosecuted. New Labour introduced a whole range of new disposals in cases involving young people, which included compelling young offenders to engage in various forms of community-based reparation. Legislation also included provisions compelling the parents of troubled children to attend counselling and 'guidance sessions'. Under New Labour, minor youth offending was used to place more and more areas of family life under the compulsory supervision of the state. This represented a significant intervention by the criminal law into family life.

The second important context for the reform around rape was New Labour's approach to justice policy. New Labour justice policy was consistently 'victim centred'. A significant aspect of the New Labour strategy was to steal the Tories' traditional ground. One aspect of this was reform of the criminal justice system. Jack Straw, Tony Blair's home secretary in 1997, indicated that he intended to 'reorientate' the justice system around the needs of victims and away from the rights of defendants. He bemoaned how the 'defendants' rights lobby' had dominated the discourse around the criminal justice system. New Labour would go on to reverse defendants' rights that had been in place for centuries. In 2003, the same year that the Sexual Offences Act was passed, the government also abolished the double-jeopardy rule, which prevented defendants from being charged with the same crime twice. The government introduced 'special measures' into criminal trials, meaning that 'vulnerable' defendants could give evidence from behind a screen or even have their evidence pre-recorded. They introduced victim impact statements, which meant that victims could give a statement about the emotional impact a crime had had on them, which could then be considered by a judge when sentencing a convicted defendant. All of these reforms represented a reorientation of the processes of justice around the emotional needs of the complainant.

It was these contexts, coupled with an outdated set of statutes, which led to the reform of the law around rape. But the changes implemented by New Labour went well beyond 'codifying' and 'modernising' the old law. In fact, the 2003 Act redefined rape in a way that would shape the next generation of rape prosecutions. To understand the significance of the changes made by New Labour, it's important to consider the discussion of a case which preceded the new law, a case involving a Royal Air Force officer called Morgan.

Morgan and the problem of honest belief

Many of the changes occasioned in 2003 were reacting to a case, *DPP v Morgan*, which, until 2003, was considered an authority on the requirements with regards to a defendant's belief in rape cases. Morgan's is a grim case. He was a senior non-commissioned officer in the Royal Air Force (RAF). He had

been out drinking with three younger RAF colleagues. After a
night out looking for women, Morgan suggested his colleagues
accompany him back to his house to have sex with his wife. His
friends were incredulous at first, but Morgan explained that
she liked kinky sex and would willingly consent to sex with all
of them. Morgan told them that any protest or disagreement
she would mount was just part of her kinky participation. The
men returned to Morgan's home where they dragged his wife
onto a double bed, before each taking turns to rape her. There
was significant dispute about what exactly was said and done
by the men in the course of the attack, but in the end all were
convicted of rape.

The men appealed their conviction by arguing that the
judge had misdirected the jury on a point of law. The judge had
told the jury, before they retired, that the defendants' 'belief in
her consent must be *reasonable*'. The men had argued before the
jury that they had all shared an honest belief that she had
consented and that there was no legal requirement to show that
their belief was 'reasonable', as the judge had suggested. The
Court of Appeal dismissed their appeal, but gave leave for
further appeal to the House of Lords on the question 'whether
in rape a defendant can properly be convicted notwithstanding
that he in fact believed the woman consented, if such belief was
not based on reasonable grounds'.

The Lords rejected the appeal, but also held that an honest,
though mistaken, belief in consent was a defence to a charge of
rape, however unlikely a reasonable man would be to hold
such a belief. The court was not really saying anything radical.
If a defendant had an honestly held but mistaken belief in
consent, then the Crown would not have proven the vital
element in any rape charge as per the law at the time: that he
intended to have intercourse without the complainant's
consent or was reckless as to whether the complainant consented. However, the case became a symbol for many of how
antiquated the law around rape had become. The drafting of
the Sexual Offences Act 2003 took place against a background

of argument around the judgement in *Morgan*, which arguably read way too much into what the judgement actually said.

The *Morgan* debate

Feminists at the time were deeply critical of the decision in *Morgan*. Professor Catherine MacKinnon argued that the judgement showed how the law treated a woman's view on her violation as entirely secondary to the judgement of a man. The courts, she claimed, were effectively saying that if a man said a woman wasn't raped, then she wasn't raped. Others took up the argument, pointing out that the case stacked the odds at a trial heavily in favour of a defendant. Morgan had shown utter disregard for his wife's wishes, yet was able to maintain his belief with complete disregard to reading his wife's signals.

Morgan was an egregious case. But hard cases make bad law. The judgement in *Morgan* was not suggesting that men could simply dismiss the views of women and form whatever view they liked about a given sexual situation. It merely said that if a defendant proved he had held an honest belief that his partner was consenting, then the Crown would have failed to prove its case on the vital point of intent. If the defendant had an honest belief in consent, he could not have intended to inflict non-consenting sex. It was in this context that others defended *Morgan* against the feminist criticism, arguing that it maintained a key liberal feature of English law: that no one will be found guilty of a crime they did not intend to commit. British academic Sara Hinchliffe saw the potential intrusion that could be occasioned by changing the law in line with feminists concerns around *Morgan*. She wrote:

> It would be a major step to argue that the law should police sexual behaviour that has never been defined as criminal, that includes no criminal intention, and that most of society would not currently see as deserving criminal penalties. Some feminists are proposing that the focus of the law should shift, towards penalizing inconsiderate behaviour. The kind of intervention into private life that would be involved is im-

mense, and the idea of having bedroom behaviour subject to criminal penalties is alarming.[2]

However, the feminist view of *Morgan* became influential in the drafting of the new law. In the course of the committee stage of the bill's passage, the committee heard argument from a steering group staffed by 'those campaigning around rape' and a number of high-profile rape-awareness feminists. This steering group argued that only actively 'communicative' sex should be considered legal and that the definition of rape should apply to a much broader spectrum of sexual activity. Sue Lees, an academic at the University of North London, argued before the committee that the distinction between rape and sex was not always clear, saying 'calling rape violence fails to address the coercive nature of some male sexual behaviour'. The steering-group members actively propagated the idea that rape and consensual sex were all part of the same spectrum, separated only by degree. They portrayed the judgement in *Morgan* as a rapist's charter, allowing men the freedom to ignore entirely the signals given off by a complainant.

The committee's report led to the drafting of the Sexual Offences Bill, which removed the defence of honestly-held belief by introducing a requirement that the defendant's belief in consent be 'reasonable'. The House of Lords, when considering the provisions of the Sexual Offences Bill that raised the 'reasonableness' requirement, pointed out that the proposed amendments to the law would seriously undermine the presumption of innocence. Lord Campbell of Alloway said of the introduction of a 'reasonableness' test:

> Those amendments of my noble friend oblige an accused to match his own characteristics with those of an abstract reasonable person in substitution for proof of his actual intent. That

---

[2]   Sarah Hinchliffe, 'Rape law reform in Britain', *Society*, May/June 2000 http://goo.gl/iBEU9A

defeats the presumption of innocence and fails wholly to miti-
gate the manifest injustice of subsection (3) of Clause 1, un-
amended, which removes the defence of honest but mistaken
belief as to consent.[3]

He went on to raise the potential injustice inherent in requiring a defendant to prove that he acted 'reasonably' in the lead-
up to sex, when there was no clear idea of what such 'reasonableness' entailed:

On the balance of what is due and fair administration, one may
well ask whether the real victim is not the person who has an
erroneous conviction. Dire consequences may follow, including
loss of his job and marriage. When he comes out of prison after
seven years, he may find that, by some method such as DNA,
he can prove that he was falsely convicted—and the Court of
Appeal may so decide. Are such men not worthy of consideration? They are the real victims of these consent cases. Let us not
overlook the concern and disappointment of the complainants
who are unable to convince the jury of their evidence. I have
sympathy for them, but one cannot disturb the entire balance of
justice to accommodate sympathy.[4]

The Lords had further criticisms of the feminist gloss on
Morgan, relating to the implication of their position with
regards to juries. One of the arguments which had been used
by feminists to critique *Morgan* was that a defendant could rely
on an unreasonable belief to 'get off' an allegation of rape. But
as Lord Berwick pointed out in the debate, this merely reflected
a grim view of the jury in rape cases:

The argument repeated so often that it is absurd for a defendant to get off on the grounds of honest belief, however unreasonable, altogether ignores the role of the jury. The simple
answer is that the defendant does not get off in such a case. I do

---

[3]   *Hansard*, 31 March 2003 http://goo.gl/EI4lwA
[4]   *Hansard*, 31 March 2003 http://goo.gl/EI4lwA

not have as much experience of rape cases as other judges, but I have some, and I have never heard of a case in which the defendant has got off on the grounds of honest belief where that belief was unreasonable. Juries are no fools. They can tell when the defendant is lying in order to put up a bogus defence. The more unreasonable the defence, the more likely it is that they will convict. If ever there were a crime where the question of guilt should be left to the good sense of juries, with the minimum of statutory interference by Parliament, it is the crime of rape.[5]

The reasonableness test was controversial throughout the passage of the bill. Respondents to the consultation on the bill remained in favour of retaining the subjective test on the ground that 'a defendant should not be criminally liable if he did not intent to commit an offence'. The Lords would later note that there was 'no evidence' that any deficiency in the conviction rate was a problem with the law. In fact, the statistics relied on by the campaigners to show that the conviction rate was 'low' would be called into serious question some seven years later with the publication of the Stern Review. The research to support the bill had been undertaken almost entirely by civil servants and had only consulted two members of the judiciary, one in Amsterdam and one in Australia. Notwithstanding the objections from the Lords and the majority of the respondents to the consultation, the Sexual Offences Act was passed into law in 2003, complete with its requirement that a defendant's belief in consent be 'reasonable'. As we will see, this 'reasonableness' requirement has become the focus of CPS reform in recent years, which has as its aim the charge and conviction of more people.

The Sexual Offences Act 2003 also created a series of 'presumptions' which would apply in certain prescribed circumstances. Where the Crown could demonstrate that one of a

---

5   *Hansard,* 31 March 2003 http://goo.gl/oTS8jd

series of circumstances were present, the court was entitled to presume that consent was absent. For example, if violence had been used in the lead-up to sex, or if a complainant had been disabled to such an extent that he or she could not communicate their consent, then the court was entitled to presume that the complainant was not consenting.

These presumptions also applied in cases involving deception. Where a complainant had been 'deceived' as to the 'nature' of the act, then the court was entitled to make a 'conclusive presumption' that the complainant had not consented. In other words, in certain circumstances, there would be nothing a defendant could do to rebut the presumption that the complainant was not consenting. Under the old law, such deception was criminalised as well. The Sexual Offences Act 1956 — which preceded the 2003 Act — made it illegal to 'procure a woman by false pretences'. However, as we will see, the character of cases under the new law are significantly broader and have even been accused of being discriminatory in their application.

The Sexual Offences Act 2003 did not only redefine rape. It expanded its reach further into the realms of sexual etiquette. This expansion has left more and more people vulnerable to a rape prosecution. Many of these new prosecutions arise in situations that many of us would find troubling, especially given that many of the cases involve those who desperately needed the authority and guidance of the people around them, rather than the blunt brute force of the law.

The regulation of sexual etiquette

The cases under the new act have shown how the courts were now becoming involved in regulating sexual etiquette. While it is right to say that there is no reliable data on the kinds of cases coming before the courts today, the cases that have come before the Court of Appeal — which is responsible for interpreting the law and issuing guidance to the lower courts — have caused significant controversy, with many suggesting that the cases show how the law around rape has expanded too far.

This was evident in the discussion around the prosecution of Benjamin Bree. Bree was a young man who had gone to visit his brother at Bournemouth University. He and his brother's flatmates had gone on a night out together and had drunk considerable amounts in the course of the evening. Among his flatmates was a girl with whom Bree had become friendly previously.

At the end of the night, they had all returned to the flat. CCTV showed Bree and the complainant returning to the flat, arm in arm. The complainant had to use a series of key fobs and keys to gain access to the flat, suggesting she was at least conscious on her return to the flat. When Bree and the complainant were back in the flat, she reacted badly to the alcohol. The men of the group were, apparently, helpful, and Bree provided the complainant with some shampoo with which to wash her hair. On the complainant's account, it was at this stage that she lost consciousness. When she came to, Bree was on top of her and giving her oral sex.

Bree was arrested the following morning. At trial, he and the complainant gave broadly similar accounts of the night. They differed about how they came to be having sex. While the complainant claimed she had passed out and awoke to Bree giving her oral sex, Bree claimed she was willing and conscious throughout. The complainant conceded that she had not said 'no' even when she realised what Bree was doing.

Bree's case effectively involved the criminal adjudication of a drunken, regrettable incident between two young people. This is, perhaps unfortunately, the sort of encounter which must happen regularly at campuses up and down the country. There was no evidence that Bree intended to commit non-consensual penetration. However, the police and the prosecuting authorities clearly took the view that the circumstances in which he engaged in sexual intercourse — with a girl who had had too much to drink — meant the circumstances in which she had given consent made it unreasonable for him to have believed she was consenting at all.

The prosecution of Benjamin Bree indicates that the courts can, today, be more active in regulating those cases where defendants arguably should have done more to obtain consent. The expansion of rape law has taken place in a context in which young people are encouraged to view these difficult, ambiguous encounters as serious incidents of sexual violence. This is supported by a legal system that has given itself the job of setting the 'reasonable' standards for sexual etiquette. The issue in Bree's case, which was later considered by the Court of Appeal in overturning his conviction, was the proper direction to be given to a jury about a complainant's capacity to consent when they have been drinking. But the fact that the case was ever brought in the first place shows the impact of the expansion of the remit of rape.

The impact of the expansion of rape law can be seen most explicitly when you consider cases involving children and those with new and emerging sexualities. While those who support the expansion of the law around rape celebrate unconditionally the fact that we can have more people convicted, it is worth considering that one of the leading cases in this area involves the prosecution of a young transgendered man, who would have done better with the help and guidance of those around him, as opposed to the ham-fisted intervention of the police and prosecution.

In 2012, a young transgendered man called McNally was jailed for two years after he was sexually intimate with a young girl before proceeding to disclose the fact that he had once been a woman. The two had built up a relationship online, in which McNally had used a male avatar. They had spoken about having children together. After McNally and the complainant had become intimate on a number of occasions, including a number of incidents of digital [finger] penetration, the complainant's mother confronted McNally accusing him of being a girl. McNally confessed. The relationship broke down, but irregular contact continued. The police became involved when the complainant's mother made a complaint to McNally's school. The school then made a complaint to the police.

The case became an authority on a doctrine known as 'rape by deception'. The Sexual Offences Act sets out a number of 'presumptions' against a defendant, which meant that in certain circumstances the defendant can be required to prove that consent existed. One such circumstance is when consent has been given on the basis of a deception. The courts have faced numerous cases in which consent has been provided following certain deceptions, and have been required to adjudicate as to whether the deception 'vitiated' the consent given by the accuser.

The issue in *McNally* was whether, by failing to disclose the fact that he had been born a girl, he had vitiated his partner's freedom to choose to sleep with him. The Court of Appeal ruled that it did and upheld his conviction. The Court of Appeal was effectively saying that McNally should have disclosed his gender history to his partner as a prerequisite for becoming sexually intimate with her.

Most people in the real world would consider the McNally case as an absurd application of rape law. The idea that a young transgendered man should be prosecuted for rape on account of failing to disclose his gender history to a girl he was fooling around with would be seen by most people as draconian in the extreme. Many, particularly feminists and those involved in activism around trans- issues, were incensed by the judgement. One commentator called the law around rape by deception a 'hetero-normative' mess.

But what these commentaries fail to acknowledge is that McNally is not unique. He will not be the last person prosecuted in circumstances that many people would find utterly wrong. McNally was arrested because he offended the state-sanctioned model of intimate life. Worse, McNally and his sexual partner—both teenagers at the time of the incident— were left marooned by the adults around them, who seemed incapable of understanding that what had happened between them was outside the boundaries of sexual violence. The case speaks not only to the expansion of the law around rape and sexual violence, but also to the crisis of intimate judgement among adults, which prevents people from taking charge of intimate situations — especially those involving young people — without the assistance of the law. It is because of the panic around rape and rape culture that McNally has served a prison sentence and is now on the Violent and Sex Offender Register (ViSOR).

Young rapists

This expansion of rape law is particularly dangerous in a society that criminalises children and young people more than ever before. Far from making us more open and engaged with youthful intimacy, educating kids about consent arrives at a time when we are less forgiving of kids who mess up in their intimate lives. In the UK between 2011 and 2013, over 300 young people were arrested for rape and sexual violence. In 2014, Greater Manchester Police released figures that suggested that they had arrested 215 children under fifteen in relation to rape allegations since 2009, some of whom were as young as eight. A 2013 report by the Children's Commissioner suggested that they had encountered 'over and over again, evidence of forced or coerced sex by young people against young people in an almost casual way'.[6] Since the passage of the law in 2003, we have annually prosecuted around 1,000 youths for offences related to sex.

When the details of these cases are reported, it becomes clear that youthful experimentation has been completely reimagined as if it were adult criminal behaviour. In each case, what might have once been called innocent experimentation has been recast as serious sexual violence. In 2010, two ten-year-olds were prosecuted at the Old Bailey — a court tradition- ally used for the most serious of adult cases — for raping an eight-year-old girl. The case had involved ambiguous sexual

---

6   'Sex without consent, I suppose that is rape': How young people in England understand sexual consent, Office of the Children's Commissioner, Novem- ber 2013

activity between the group of children, which the defence described as a game of 'I'll show you mine, you show me yours'. When the two boys were convicted of attempted rape, they were placed on the sex offenders' register. Many were outraged by the case, saying that it showed the 'barbarity of our courts system' and that 'in no other jurisdiction in the world would youthful fumbling be interpreted as rape', but few pointed out that the case is the natural end point for a system of law around rape which has encouraged the criminal-isation of what would previously have been considered relatively ordinary aspects of intimate behaviour.

The Sexual Offences Act 1993 abolished the presumption that boys aged between ten and thirteen were not capable of having sexual intercourse.[7] *Doli incapax*, the presumption that children could not form criminal intent, was abolished five years later. Together, these two changes meant that children could now be found to fulfil all the requisite ingredients for a rape charge. Such prosecutions began almost immediately. In the same year that *doli incapax* was abolished, a twelve-year-old boy became the youngest boy ever at that time to be prosecuted for rape having climbed on top of his five-year-old niece, saying he was 'going to do what mummies and daddies do'. In 1997, a ten-year-old boy was convicted of indecent assault at the same court, having been charged with the rape of a twelve-year-old boy. Given that children were already vulnerable to prosecution under the old law, it is not surprising that they are prosecuted more readily under the new law, which is far harsher when dealing with cases involving difficult and ambiguous activity between young people.

Many people pointed out that the above cases, as well as those involving McNally and Bree, were examples of how the law on rape has gone wrong. But few recognised that these cases arise in a wider context, in which matters of intimacy and sex are seen as subjects for official intervention and adjudica-

---

[7]   Sexual Offences Act 1993 http://goo.gl/g13k7t

tion like never before. The panic around rape culture does not seek to reclaim these vital spheres of human experience and judgement from the state. Instead, it invites the state to become even more involved in such matters. It actively encourages more prosecutions of children, drunk students and transgendered people for violating the state-sanctioned model of consent. Worse, it leaves us less and less capable of making judgements about those difficulties in intimate life that we might face, including those cases involving children and young people.

Conclusion

Far from 'ignoring' rape, rape-law reform has made prosecuting rape easier. The crime of rape has changed significantly since the passage of the new law and the CPS now prosecutes many cases which we, as members of the public, may be worried about. Should a young trans man be prosecuted for failing to disclose his gender history? Should a ten-year-old be prosecuted for childish experimentation? Should we really lock up students who have regrettable drunken flings with one another? All of the above have been condoned as falling squarely within the contemporary ambit of modern rape law.

We have seen how the reality of rape is far removed from what is portrayed by those who argue we live in a rape culture. Far from minimising or ignoring rape, the law has expanded dramatically to include far more sexual behaviour. This occurred concurrently with an expansion of the law into other areas of our intimate lives. The climate of misinformation which flows around the contemporary debate on rape fails entirely to capture the fact that intimate life is now awash with new standards and controls, of which rape law is just one part. The final two chapters turn to the impact that the argument that we live in a 'rape culture' is having on three key areas: intimacy, freedom and justice.

Four

The Impact
of Rape Panic

We have considered in some detail the facts about rape. We have seen that, contrary to the idea that we live in a society that trivialises or minimises sexual violence, rape law has expanded significantly over recent decades against a background of state interference in many aspects of intimate life. The absurd moral panic around rape and rape culture has given rise to a litany of misinformation about rape, particularly in the context of the justice system.

In the chapters that follow we will consider the impact that a climate of panic is having on the way we deal with rape cases and the way we live our intimate lives. Firstly, we will consider a brief history of the rape culture argument, which has always sought to cultivate and maintain a damaging sense of vulnerability among those who believe in it. We will then consider how the panic around rape leads to a hysterical, unthinking and often inhumane response to rape cases. The panic around rape, coupled with the belief in an insidious rape 'culture', leads some to advocate the abandonment of some key principles of Western civilisation when confronted with rape cases.

Secondly, we will see how the 'rape culture' argument is antithetical to freedom. It is deeply censorious and encourages intolerance of any attitude that is seen to offend or even challenge the contemporary consensus around rape. It also encourages both men and women to be constantly deferential to female vulnerability, which has the perverse effect of placing significant power in the hands of men to govern the terms of women's sex lives.

Lastly, in the chapter that follows, we will see how the rape-culture argument has given rise to its own form of justice, one that prioritises the validation and confirmation of individual experience above the objective establishment of the truth. Not only does the argument that we live in a 'rape culture' threaten our capacity to negotiate our intimate lives independently, it also destroys our capacity to deal objectively and effectively with actual allegations of criminality in the intimate setting. Given that one of the key allegations of the rape-culture argument is that the justice system cannot cope with rape, it is, in many ways, a self-fulfilling prophecy.

The fearful narcissism of rape culture

An important element in explaining why the argument that we live in a rape culture survives today is understanding that it is a worldview which encourages a deep sense of vulnerability in its adherents. The idea that films, pop songs and off-the-cuff remarks can all 'normalise' the crime of rape is an expression of deep distrust and isolation. It suggests that the people around us are incapable of hearing certain lyrics without being encouraged to rape. It suggests that banal and childish misogyny is capable of affecting people's view of women to such an extent that they become more likely to commit horrific crimes. It encourages us to believe that numerous aspects of our everyday lives are symptomatic of something deeply sinister, rendering us all inherently and constantly vulnerable to sexual violence.

When I started looking at the history of the phrase 'rape culture', I quickly saw that there was little to find. The literature around the topic is often uncertain and conflicting. A debate rages among those who use the phrase about where it actually comes from. Some claim it is lifted from the title of a 1970s film about black prison inmates forming a rape-awareness group, but this claim is merely made on the basis that this was apparently the first time the phrase was explicitly used.[1]

There are, in fact, traces of the rape culture argument throughout the twentieth century. In her superb history of rape, Joanna Bourke describes how a belief that certain environments compel their inhabitants to sexual violence has often been used to generate panic and fear about a particular section of society.[2] Arguably, in the twentieth century, none felt the force of this prejudice more than black men, who have periodically been described as having been turned to rape by the baseness of their 'culture', which has been consistently des-cribed as encouraging sexual competition and degrading to women. Bourke cites Winfield Collins, a racist apologist, who wrote in a 1905 pamphlet justifying lynching that:

> Two of the negro's most prominent characteristics are the utter lack of chastity and complete ignorance of veracity. The negro's sexual laxity, considered so immoral or even criminal in the white man's civilisation, may have been all but a virtue in the habit of his origin.[3]

If the language of the argument sounds familiar, it's because his language is still used in discussing rape today. Here, in the writings of a racist apologist, is the logic of the contemporary rape culture argument. For Collins, a black man was compelled to rape by the 'habits of his origin', which encouraged sexual laxity and loose morals. Today, the rape culture argument encourages the same view that Collins had of black men — that they were primitive, brutish and constantly prone to influence by 'habits of origin' — about all young men, especially those from traditionally masculine environments.

---

[1]   See for example, Carrie N. Baker, *The women's movement against sexual harassment*, Cambridge University Press, 2008, page 41
[2]   Joanna Bourke, *Rape: A History from 1860 to the Present*
[3]   Ibid.

The fearfulness and panic inherent in the idea of rape culture made it effective at stoking hatred at times of deep social division. The Ku Klux Klan deployed the rape culture argument to justify extreme racism. My editor at *Spiked*, Brendan O'Neill, has noted how the hysteria generated around rape by the KKK bears similarities to the panic around rape today:

> One of the main ways in which racists there (in the American South) maintained social divisions and social order was through the spectre of rape. They promoted the idea that white women were under constant threat from 'lustful black men'. Even though the black rape of white women was not a major problem, still the idea that there was a menacing culture of rape was indulged. [4]

It is easy to see the appeal of the rape culture argument to violent racists. It utterly dehumanises its targets by portraying them as blind, unthinking recipients of the degraded culture that they inhabit. The KKK used the rape culture argument to portray blacks as lacking the rational ability to control their 'lusts', which social commentators had — for years before them — portrayed as part and parcel of black culture. The panicked idea that young black men were turned base by their culture lasted well into the twentieth century. Bourke quotes the following passage from criminologist Menachem Amir, who is still widely cited for his work on rape prevalence:

> Negro lower class subculture embodies all the characteristics of a lower class subculture but has some of its features in a more pronounced form. The negro subculture is characterized by the revolving of life around some basic 'focal concerns' which include a search for thrills through aggressive actions and sexual exploits. The emphasis is given by males to masculinity,

---

4   The War on Rape: the logic of the lynch mob returns, *Spiked*, 15 December 2014 http://goo.gl/A32OvO

and their need to display it through brief and transitory relations with women[5].

Here again is the logic of the rape culture argument. Certain cultures, according to both Collins and Amir, encourage and propagate rape through 'focal concerns' combined with rapacious and competitive sexual appetites. While these views undoubtedly betrayed their authors' prejudices about the 'culture' they were talking about, which they took to be sexually lax and falling short of the morality displayed in other areas of society, they also communicated a denigrated view of the people who inhabited that culture, who were portrayed as being blindly compelled to rape by the environments they found themselves in.

The argument that people were driven to rape by their environments was common throughout the twentieth century. Bourke describes how different minority groups have come to be blamed for the prevalence of rape at different stages in modern history: 'adolescent thugs, impoverished men, male immigrants and men viewed as unattractive' have, at different points in the modern history of rape, been singled out as primarily responsible for its prevalence. Bourke attributes this to a middle-class attempt to deflect attention away from their own social class, and to portray rape as something which was done by other people, out there in some other base and uncivilised 'culture'.

Of course, the racist dynamic that propelled the rape culture argument in the past does not apply in today's context. However, what these arguments have in common with the rape culture arguments of today is that they are both portray people as culturally determined. The view of contemporary rape culture encourages a diminished view of people in order to portray them as constantly susceptible to manipulation by the 'culture' they see around them. While the racists of the past

---

5   Quoted in Bourke, op cit.

restricted their argument to minority groups, as part of their stoking up of racial hatred, contemporary rape culture adherents encourage this debased and deterministic view of everyone in society. They argue that we are all susceptible to influence by our environments, much in the same way that Amir and Collins thought blacks were corruptible by their 'origins' or 'culture'. We will also see that contemporary rape culture adherents, much like the racist users of the rape culture argument in the past, similarly encourage an abandonment of moral perspective and due process when dealing with rape cases. These characteristics are shared between the racist fear-mongers of the past and the feminist fear-mongers of today.

The starting point for the 'rape culture' argument in its modern form can be found in the writings of rape-awareness campaigner and feminist Susan Brownmiller. In 1974 Brownmiller published *Against Our Will*, which was to become one of the key texts of the emerging movement around rape awareness.[6] Brownmiller has since become known as one of the most 'militant' feminists of the second wave of feminism, which emerged in Britain and America in the 1970s and 80s. Brownmiller argued that men are not compelled to rape merely by their culture, but by their biology. Brownmiller believed that men were biologically determined to rape women and that women were forever doomed to be victims of men's domination. She referred to 'cultural factors'—like the existence of pornography and sexist lyrics in pop songs—not as symptoms of a rape culture, but rather as symptomatic of man's biological determination to rape. While Brownmiller never uses the phrase 'rape culture', her argument is that a patriarchal society, in which rape is the norm, inevitably gives rise to a culture in which 'anti-female propaganda' like pornography and sexist cultural narratives can thrive.

The term 'rape culture' has been developed among a particular strain of feminists who were heavily influenced by

---

[6]   Susan Brownmiller, *Against Our Will: Men, Women and Rape*

Brownmiller's arguments regarding man's biological determinism towards rape. Later writers developed the phrase 'rape culture' as a means of describing a society in which women were condemned to biological vulnerability and which cultivated laws and practices that institutionalised their status as victims. Diane Herman, writing in the 1980s, used the term 'rape culture' to describe how rape and sex were on a single continuum of dominant behaviour:

> Because of the aggressive–passive, dominant–submissive, me-Tarzan-you-Jane nature of the relationship between the sexes in our culture, there is a close association between violence and sexuality... 'fuck you' is meant as a brutal attack in verbal terms ... pacifism seems suspiciously effeminate. Thus it is very difficult for our society to distinguish rape from normal heterosexual relations. Indeed, our culture can be defined as a rape culture because the image of heterosexual intercourse is based on a rape model of sexuality.[7]

Later writers adopted Brownmiller's argument about biological determinism and used it to explain the cultural structures which existed throughout society. Andrea Dworkin, who became known as a particularly 'militant' advocate of women's perennial victimhood, wrote in 1991 that:

> The fact of the matter is that the basic premise about women is that we are born to be fucked. That is it. Now that means a lot of things. For a lot of years it meant that marriage was outright ownership of a woman's body and intercourse was a right of marriage. That meant that intercourse was, *per se*, an act of force. Because the power of the state mandated that the woman accept intercourse. She belonged to the man. The cultural remnants of this is that in our society, men experience intercourse as possession of women. The culture talks about intercourse as conquering women. Women surrendering. Women being

---

7   Diane Herman, *The Rape Culture* http://goo.gl/362QbM

taken. We are looking at a paradigm for rape. Not at a paradigm for reciprocity, for equality, for mutuality or for freedom.[8]

The notion of vulnerability to rape at this time was supported, to some degree, by objective truth. For women writing in the 1970s and '80s, there were real societal forces to battle against which prevented the effective prosecution of rape. So much has been written about the law around rape that it has become trite to say that the law, for centuries, reflected the status of women as the property of men. In the early twentieth century, rape was seen as an anomalous perversion, carried out predominantly by the mentally ill. The superb book *Real Rape* by Susan Estrich details some of the barriers that faced women seeking to have their case prosecuted in these decades.[9] These included the archaic marital exemption, which meant that men could rape their wives without ever being prosecuted, and absurd laws around recent complaint that meant that a woman would be ignored if she took longer than twenty-four hours to raise her complaint with the police. Estrich and others produced an abundance of evidence that rape was dealt with poorly by each and every level of the justice system for a long period of time.

It is similarly trite to say that today things are far from perfect. Police officers continue to be negligent, prosecutors continue to make mistakes and prejudices still exist. But the argument around 'rape culture' survives notwithstanding the enormous social change that has occurred since the argument's inception. Today, as we have seen, prosecutors are desperate to prosecute rape in the most public way possible. A small army of specially trained police officers deal with every aspect of rape allegations. The rules around rape trials have radically changed to make the experience of going to court easier. Of course, today's system is not perfect, but the changes that have occurred around rape have been extremely wide ranging. This

---

[8]   Andrea Dworkin, *Terror, Torture and Resistance* http://goo.gl/A7UDmI
[9]   Susan Estrich, *Real Rape*, Harvard University Press

fact is completely ignored by the adherents of the rape culture argument, who will use misleading and inaccurate statistics to attempt to present the world in the same terms as the feminists of the 1970s and '80s.

It is notable that today, in an age where rape laws enable prosecutions for an enormous spectrum of activity and the prosecuting authorities actually boast about their ability to 'drive up' the numbers of people charged and convicted, groups who purport to campaign against 'rape culture' often resist defining it altogether, instead offering a seemingly endless list of examples. For example, the campaign group Force, whose stated aim is campaigning against the rape culture, says:

> Rape culture includes jokes, TV music, advertising, legal jargon, laws, words and imagery that make violence against women and sexual coercion seem so normal that people believe that rape is inevitable. Rather than viewing the culture of rape as a problem to change, people in a rape culture think about the persistence of rape as 'just the way things are'.[10]

Where the feminists of the past were able to identify objective political realities that prevented the prosecution of rape, today the absence of those realities, the bare fact that more and more people are being prosecuted for rape than ever before[11] means that those who are convinced we live in a rape culture have to create their own realities, which seek to replicate the vulnerabilities of women in the past. In the absence of real social factors making women more vulnerable to rape, those who believe in a rape culture end up ascribing the same power to a gyrating Robin Thicke that feminists of the past ascribed to sexist laws and practices that evidently made prosecuting rape harder.

---

[10]   Force's website is available here: http://goo.gl/Gk0NHv
[11]   *Violence against Women and Girls Crime Report 2015* Crown Prosecution Service

This is why today's argument that we live in rape culture reflects a deeply personal, subjective conception of what constitutes 'culture'. This is evident in the academic writing on rape culture that emerged in the 1990s. This writing gave rise to a personal and subjective conception of what constitutes culture, which effectively allowed anything to be included in the description of rape culture if a particular person experienced it as such. In the 1990s, the term 'rape culture' became the subject of a collection of essays, titled *Transforming a Rape Culture*.[12] Each essay is highly personal, exploring how each of the writers experience certain phenomena. In Bell Hooks's essay, she explains how 'rape culture' affected her taste in men, compelling her to prefer aggressive traditionally masculine sexual partners. In another essay within the collection, the writer complains how her experience of certain language — including the aggressive connotations of the word 'fuck' — made her constantly aware of the threat of rape. By the end of the 1990s, the focus of 'rape culture' was no longer about actual 'culture', or things that existed outside of people's heads; rather, it became about individual experiences of vulnerability in what was perceived to be an inherently threatening world.

Today, the very act of defining rape culture often mirrors this individuated, atomised interpretation of 'culture'. In February 2015, the writer Zerlina Maxwell launched a Twitter hashtag '#rapecultureis' and invited people to list (yet more) examples of what they thought were symptoms of rape culture. The examples included a Republican politician in Montana trying to pass a bill banning the wearing of 'provocative' yoga trousers to the claim that only three percent of American rape defendants eventually receive a custodial sentence. The suggestion was, presumably, that the same thing, this elusive 'rape culture', could govern both the prejudices of criminal juries and the sartorial prejudices of American politicians. Of course, no one in the Twittersphere denied that any of these

---

[12]   Buchwald Roth and Fletcher, *Transforming a Rape Culture*, 1995

examples could count as 'rape culture', precisely because the term itself is without a fixed meaning. Defining it en masse was perfectly illustrative of the non-specific and subjective nature of the phrase's contemporary meaning. It can mean whatever you want it to mean.

The argument that we live in a 'rape culture' is not about 'culture' at all, but the way that people view the world. It is fundamentally an expression of inherent vulnerability. While few would necessarily adopt Susan Brownmiller's position, that men are biologically determined to rape and that women remain eternally and inherently vulnerable, it is from this model of sex and intimacy that the argument that we live in a rape culture arises. It still conceives of women as inherently vulnerable, and of unregulated and private interaction as fundamentally risky and potentially harmful. The reason that the argument around rape culture survives really has nothing to do with rape, and everything to do with how we view ourselves in the uncertain world of human interaction.

Researching rape culture

Recent writers on rape culture have drawn heavily on the work of academics to support their beliefs. In doing so, they often obliterate, exaggerate and misrepresent the nature of the research they are discussing. While the discussion of this research is the subject of others' books, we should consider how academic research is used by those who believe in a rape culture to support their argument.

In academia, significant energy has been expended on demonstrating the existence of 'rape myths'. This research has focused on demonstrating misogynistic attitudes within the police force, the judiciary and among jurors that many have argued prevent rape from being successfully prosecuted[13]. Some scholars have described this focus within the research as a 'shift

---

[13]   Miranda Horvath, Jennifer Brown (eds), *Rape: Challenging Contemporary Thinking*, Routledge

to attitudes' in explaining the failures of the justice system to cope with rape[14].

This research is subject to lengthy and engaging debate elsewhere. But, for our purposes, it is worthwhile to consider how the rape culture proponents use the discussion around rape myths to their own ends. Firstly, rape culture proponents will assert without reliable evidence that the persistence of certain ideas about rape is connected to cultural phenomena. They will say that it is people's interactions with a fundamentally misogynistic culture which forms their 'rape supportive' attitudes and, in an even greater logical leap, that such rape-supportive attitudes make them more likely to actually rape.

There is a significant gap between what the research finds and what the rape culture proponents claim that it finds. Rape myth research uses a particular scale to determine the extent of people's beliefs in certain ideas around rape. These include whether an invite for coffee after a date amounts to an 'invitation for sex' or whether someone wearing a short skirt is indicating a greater willingness to engage in sexual activity. Believing these things does not necessarily make a person more likely to do awful things, just as the absence of such an attitude does not prevent someone from doing awful things. It arguably does not even make them more likely to acquit a defendant in particular circumstances. While the research makes narrow claims about the existence of certain ideas among members of the public, rape myth proponents use these claims as a means of characterising the whole of society as 'rape supportive'.

Even if everything that the rape myth proponents said was right – and there is a great deal to say about why they are wrong – there is still no evidence that people are determined by their attitudes or that attitudes are determined strictly by interactions with a 'misogynist culture'. Academic research has consistently failed to demonstrate the link between pornography, computer games, music videos and other cultural

---

14   H. Reece, op cit

phenomena and the prevalence of sexual violence. People's views on isolated questions are relevant, but not determinative of how they will act in a given set of circumstances. In their use of academic research, rape culture proponents attempt to give academic credibility to ideas which are completely divorced from reality.

In America, rape culture is said to be found in sexually aggressive environments. For the past two decades, research into bars and clubs has explored the nature of sexually aggressive environments, identifying the perpetrators and positing causes[15]. As well as numerous nightclubs and bars, fraternity houses on American campuses have similarly been subject to analysis with regards to their tendency to produce 'sexually aggressive' behaviour[16].

But the use of this research to demonstrate the existence of a rape culture merely demonstrates how the term is so broad as to be meaningless. In her book, *The Alarming Rise of Rape Culture*, Kate Harding uses this research to claim that Western society does not view rape as a serious crime[17]. Of course, on both sides of the Atlantic, nothing could be further than the truth. Rape is one of the most stigmatised criminal offences, as we have seen in examples throughout this book. The jump from the claims of the research – that sexual aggression takes on a particular character in bar-room settings and that certain people hold certain views about sex – to arguing that the whole of the US and the UK 'minimises' or normalises sexual violence shows how willing the rape culture proponents are to play fast and loose with research.

---

[15]   See Kathryn Graham *et al*, 'Blurred Lines? Sexual aggression and barroom culture', *Alcoholism: Clinical and Experimental Research*, May 2014 http://goo.gl/m0jq6a

[16]   See for example 'Fraternities and Collegiate Rape Culture: Why Are Some Fraternities More Dangerous Places for Women?' *Gender and Society*, 1 April 1996, Vol.10(2), pp.133-147

[17]   Kate Harding, *The Alarming Rise of Rape Culture and what we can do about it*, De Cop Lifelong Books, 2015

At the risk of sounding trite, we hardly need academics to tell us that people can still be sexist. We don't need to study seedy bars to know that the men in them are likely to be seedy. I don't need an academic to tell me that, in bars across the world, women run the risk of being touched in bars by sexist men. But equally, I don't need to be a criminologist to know that these studies say nothing about the existence of a rape culture. In fact, by presenting the existence of creepy, touchy-feely men as evidence of a 'rape culture', it is these writers which detract from the seriousness of rape. They are the ones who argue that unwanted touching in a nightclub can be meaningfully compared to sexual violence.

The rape culture argument takes isolated evidence of sexist attitudes and behaviour and ties it together under the enormous umbrella of 'rape culture'. Whatever the value of the academic research in this area, its conclusions are used by rape culture proponents to give their position the veneer of academic respectability. Of course, few academics working on rape would ever use the term rape culture, precisely because it manipulates and distorts their conclusions into oblivion.

Rape culture and moral perspective

A number of recent cases have shown how the argument that we live in a rape culture encourages an abandonment of some key principles in our discussion around rape. Rape is a crime that requires a principled and reasoned response. The dividing lines drawn by the law are inevitably narrow and demand nuanced and considered discussion around their application. The rape culture argument encourages the opposite of this approach. Its fearful and panicked starting point means its adherents are often pushed to violent and unthinking responses to individual cases. This is shown most clearly in the argument that individual cases should be used to 'send a message' about rape to wider society, which is a position often voiced by those who believe we live in a rape culture. These responses reflect the aggressive defensiveness of the rape culture adherents, a defensiveness which is understandable when you consider that their approach to these cases is one rooted in their own vulnerability and fear.

This was shown starkly following a recent case in the town of Steubenville, Ohio in the United States. On 11 August 2012, a sixteen-year-old girl, who was unconscious from alcohol, was sexually assaulted by two high-school American football players. Both defendants were sixteen at the time of the incident. The perpetrators circulated widely footage and photographs from the incident that went on to form the bulk of the case against them. The boys were eventually convicted. One, Trent Mays, was sentenced to at least two years in the state juvenile system; the other, Ma'lik Richmond, was sentenced to at least one year.[18] Both faced the prospect of being held until they were twenty-one, at the discretion of the authorities, although Richmond was released after nine months.[19]

Commentators immediately used the fact that the boys were involved in American football to show how traditional masculine environments were a breeding ground for rape culture. One commentator, writing in *Forbes* magazine, said that the case showed how 'jock culture morphs into rape culture'.[20] Another called Steubenville 'Rape Culture's Abu Ghraib moment', as if a case involving a group of teenagers had shone a light on the sexual brutality of the adult world.[21] Many commentators drew attention to the fact that Steubenville life revolved around football, with many of the young men achieving success solely through their participation in sport. For rape culture proponents, this small group of men

---

[18]   Ohio Teenagers Guilty in Rape That Social Media Brought to Light, *New York Times*, 17 March 2013 http://goo.gl/1KGPES

[19]   Ma'lik Richmond, convicted in Steubenville rape case, released from juvenile detention, *New York Daily News*, 6 January 2014 http://goo.gl/meQdOW

[20]   Lesson From Steubenville Trial: How Jock Culture Morphs Into Rape Culture, *Forbes*, 17 March 2013 http://goo.gl/6qejXj

[21]   Laurie Penny on Steubenville: this is rape culture's Abu Ghraib moment, *New Statesman*, 19 March 2013 http://goo.gl/sq5O3

became a symbol of how football culture creates a breeding ground for sexual violence across the adult world.

The need to use such a tragic case to make a political point led certain commentators to be utterly unforgiving of the convicted boys, some going so far as to bemoan the fact that many outlets referred to the conviction of the boys as a 'tragic waste' of their talents on the field. This was a classic example of 'rape culture', some said, because it minimised the suffering of the victim in favour of mourning the tragedy of punishment upon the perpetrator. By focusing on the 'tragedy' inherent in the boys' lost potential, society tacitly acknowledged that what happened to the victim was utterly normal and barely capable of mention.

The treatment of the Steubenville case showed a degree of navel-gazing narcissism inherent in the rape culture argument, which leads to a complete loss of moral perspective. Of course, the case was a tragedy for all involved. The victim will be forced to live with the incident for the rest of her life and deserves all the sympathy and support that she requires. But one key fact seemed to be ignored by the rape culture commentariat in their discussion of this case, one that betrayed their own loss of moral perspective. The case they were talking about involved children. Throughout the rape culture-orientated commentary on the case, the boys involved were often referred to as 'evil' and 'barbaric'. Very few pieces that cited the case as example of 'rape culture' mentioned the boys' ages.

The narcissism inherent in the rape culture argument means that these commentators are incapable of making the nuanced moral distinctions that are vital in our contemporary discussion around rape. In the vast majority of cases, we recognise that it is a mark of civility in news reporting that we regard the moral transgressions of the young as a 'tragic waste'. In an age in which young people are criminalised more than ever in history, particularly in the UK, we should welcome the fact that the media retain some perspective on these defendants, rather than dismissing them as evil and comparing them to adult war criminals.

The narcissism of the rape culture argument was also evident in the discussion around English footballer Ched Evans. Evans, as we have discussed before, was convicted in circumstances that many people questioned. There were many people involved in the discussion around Evans who did not think that the law of rape should cover the kind of behaviour that Evans was guilty of. Personally, I do not find the fact of Evans's conviction particularly troubling. I do not think it represents the worst example of the application of the law around rape and, subject to his right of appeal and his protestations of innocence, I am not overly troubled by the fact that he received a lengthy prison sentence.

However, his treatment on release demonstrated how the rape culture adherents were willing to engage in the lowest form of mob justice in defence of their worldview. Once he was released, Evans attempted to return to professional football. The judge, in sentencing Evans, had not thought it fit to prevent him from playing the game professionally. There was no legal impediment to him doing so and no one involved in the case made any argument that his conviction should prevent him from pursuing his career.

However, for those promoting the notion that we live in a rape culture, allowing Evans to return to the 'beautiful game' was too much. In August 2014, following his release, a petition was launched to prevent him playing for his old club, Sheffield United. The petition claimed that allowing Evans to play professional football 'would be an insult to the woman who was raped and to all women like her who have suffered at the hands of a rapist'. The petition received in excess of 60,000 signatures. High-profile sponsors of the club threatened to withdraw funds if Evans was allowed to play. While the court determined his legal sentence, one which was deemed commensurate with the offence he was convicted of, the panic around rape allowed for the imposition of an extra-judicial punishment, which sought to prevent him returning to his normal life. Sheffield United backed down in the face of the furore and refused to sign Evans.

Evans's extra-judicial punishment did not end there. In January 2015, Oldham Athletic sought to sign Evans. On 7 January, the chairman at Oldham indicated that Evans would form part of the team for the coming weekend's fixtures. Immediately, the Twittersphere swung into action. A further online petition was launched against Evans playing for Oldham. The club board reported that threats were made by Evans's detractors to members of the club's staff and their families. Eventually, Oldham was forced into dropping Evans, too.

Those who campaigned against Evans claimed they were merely giving voice to public opinion. But there was no broad agreement in the public about how Evans should be treated. In fact, those who mobilised against him tended to hold grim views about the public at large, particularly those involved in watching football. Time and time again, commentators emphasised that allowing Evans to play would lead to him being seen as a 'role model' among young people, who would come to idolise him both for his footballing ability and for his sexual violence. When I heard this argument in the discussion around Evans, I would ask what these people thought of the parents of the young people they were talking about. Did they have no role in influencing what aspect of Evans their children came to respect? Was it not at least possible that football fans would in fact give Evans a particularly hard time in light of his conviction? The argument that Evans would be unquestioningly welcomed back to football, notwithstanding his conviction, and would quickly be idolised by those watching the game—especially the young—suggested that those mobilising against Evans actually held deep contempt for the judgement and conscience of the very members of the public that they were claiming to represent.

The narcissism encouraged by the argument that we live in a rape culture is summed up in three words: 'send a message'. For those who believe in a rape culture, the treatment of those convicted of rape needs to 'send a message' to wider society in order to counteract the toxic effects of the rape culture. While Evans attempted to return to football, an article by high-profile columnist Caitlin Moran appeared in *The Times*, in which she wrote:

> Perhaps young, rich, fit, unrepentant men who have raped *do* need to see their lives reduced to ash—without prospect of forgiveness, employment or absolution—until the day they die. I'm starting to see the sense in choosing, say, a hundred rapists and making their lives publicly, endlessly awful— unrelentingly humiliating, without prospect of absolution. Of making them famous for being appalling; regarded as untouchable. So that men become terrified of raping, in the same way women are terrified of being raped. So that rapists spend their lives dealing with the night they raped in the same way women currently do.[22]

The idea was that the normal rules of society, by which we tend to allow people the space to live their lives as they choose within the limits of the law, should not apply to a certain kind of offender. Instead, they should be made subject to an extra-judicial form of mob rule. There, in black and white, was the barbaric heart of the rape-culture argument. We will see that this abandonment of objectivity, impartiality and judgement has come to be reflected in the rise of a new form of justice around contemporary rape allegations. First, we should consider the impact of the rape culture argument on our freedom to live with one another.

Rape culture and freedom

The fact that the 'rape culture' is underpinned by a deep sense of vulnerability explains why the argument is used to vilify particular ways of life, which are seen as 'offensive' or trigger-

---

[22]   The limits of redemption, *The Times*, 13 December 2014 http://goo.gl/hWUolI

ing. One particular target has been what is known today as 'lad culture'. The rape culture argument routinely treats traditional masculine culture as a breeding ground for rape and sexual violence. In the 1970s and '80s, this was expressed in academia through the relentless examination of 'frat houses' at US colleges, in an attempt to demonstrate the link between close male association and rape.

This obsession with close male association leads to junk reporting and pseudoscience. Early in 2015, reports began to emerge of a study that purported to demonstrate that 'one in three college men would rape a woman if they could get away with it'. According to the majority of reports of the study, men who showed an intention to force women to have sex did not necessarily support the idea that they would rape a woman, suggesting that young men did not see forced sex as rape.

But this study was quickly shown to be merely the latest in the long string of nonsense studies written about American campuses. The study had only surveyed eighty-six men, only seventy-six of whose responses were actually used in the final analysis. Of those men included in the results, twenty-three said they had 'intentions to force a woman to sexual inter-course' and nine said that they would 'rape a woman' if they could get away with it. Considering that the average university in the US has a student population of around 15,000, finding out that a few of those students would commit a rape if they could get away with it is, as one commentator said, just as likely to be an indication that a few of the 'students didn't take the survey too seriously' as it is an indication of a serious problem with campus sexual assault.[23]

Recently, the alleged connection between lad culture and rape culture has been used as a justification for further inter-vention into networks of male association. Many commentators both in the UK and the US have asked whether now is the time

---

[23]   No, we did not just learn 1 in 3 college men would rape if they could get away with it, *Washington Examiner*, 13 January 2015 http://goo.gl/ZOJHLl

to ban fraternities entirely, notwithstanding the fact that there is no reliable evidence that being a member of a fraternity makes you more likely to commit any act of sexual violence. One commentator, bemoaning the overly restrictive approach of tackling 'solely criminal acts of rape' said:

> Why should we fear talking about the socialization process by which boys and men are trained to see themselves as powerful over women and to see women as sexual objects? Why should we fear asking critical questions about all-male spaces, such as athletic teams and fraternities, where these attitudes might be reinforced?[24]

This obsession with private male association illustrates the narcissism of the rape culture argument. There is no reliable evidence that membership of an athletic team or a fraternity leads to becoming a rapist. But what offends the rape culture proponents is not the possibility that these frat guys and footballers would actually do anything in the real world. Rather, the problem for the rape culture proponents is that these groups are developing 'attitudes' which they find obnoxious and unpleasant. The narcissism of the rape culture argument creates a deeply censorious impulse, one that seeks to cleanse the world of any immature or obnoxious opinion that could be thought to intrude on one's sense of self-worth.

This has become manifest in the UK, particularly in relation to students. The National Union of Students (NUS) held an inaugural 'anti lad culture' summit in 2014, in which students were encouraged to 'eradicate' lad culture from their campuses. The London School of Economics Rugby Club was forcibly disbanded by the LSE student union in October 2014 for distributing 'misogynistic' material as promotion for its club night. In response, the rugby club launched a 'Good Lad' campaign, in which the rugby players paraded themselves

---

[24]   Rape, rape culture and the problem of patriarchy, *Waging Non Violence*, 29 April 2014 http://goo.gl/cfPWcA

outside the university buildings, inviting people to have their photo taken with a sign having completed the sentence 'A good lad is ...'. The intolerance of lad culture shows that today, the argument that we live in a rape culture is often used to justify petty authoritarianism, which — in turn — is symptomatic of the argument's narcissistic and self-centred heart. As well as encouraging its adherents to be constantly aware and vigilant about their own vulnerability, it also encourages them to be ruthlessly intolerant when it comes to protecting themselves from anything that could be seen to damage their self-esteem.

Sexual freedom

While portraying groups of men as savages in need of reining in, the rape culture argument also portrays women as incapable of negotiating their sex lives for themselves. There is no better example of this than the truly bizarre movement in the US which encourages 'bystander intervention' to prevent rape and sexual assault. This movement involves a number of organisations, including prominent anti-rape campaign groups, who aim to teach men how to protect women from unwanted sex by 'intervening' when she has had 'too much to drink' or where she cannot say no to a man who is being 'a jerk'. The campaign group Men Can Stop Rape is one such organisation, whose posters encourage young men to 'get an authority', like a bouncer, to break up situations he thinks may lead to sexual assault. Other posters encourage men to stop a woman buying another drink if he thinks she will become too drunk to know what she is doing in the bedroom, and even to order her a taxi if she is talking to a bothersome man.[25]

In other words, the campaign encourages men to behave like Victorian chaperones, constantly keeping an eye on their female friends, before 'intervening' like a jealous cuckold to prevent anything they think the woman might regret. Some contemporary feminists have rejected the 'bystander interven-

---

[25]   Resources on bystander intervention can be found at mencanstoprape.org

tion' movement, seeing it as placing too much power in the 'hands of the powerful' over women's lives. Of course this is true, if you assume men are inherently 'powerful'. But what they fail to see is that the movement is the logical conclusion of the degraded view of women as perpetual victims that is inherent in the notion of 'rape culture'. The more you see women as inherently vulnerable to rape in virtue of their biology, the more you will seek to have the strong, chivalrous man assume responsibility for her sex life.

The rape culture argument is in fact developing into an all-out assault on female sexual autonomy. In a recent interview, author Camille Paglia pointed out how the rape culture movement was reverting women back to their position as doted upon and sexually passive. Paglia first argued in the 1960s that the 'freedom to risk rape' is one of the fundamental freedoms contemporary women should embrace. In 2015, she reiterated the argument in an interview with *Reason* magazine. She called dating a 'dangerous sport', but that attempting to 'legislate for what happens on dates' would seriously limit the ability of both men and women to exercise any degree of autonomy whatsoever.[26]

Paglia is a powerful advocate for freedom against the paternalism of the rape culture argument. You may disagree with Paglia's strong language, but her argument goes to the heart about what the rape culture argument, and the fundamental cultural narcissism which provides its force, does to contemporary intimacy. Paglia's point brings out the key fact about intimacy: the fact that it is risky. 'Danger' she says, 'is the drama of love'. Without risk, genuine intimacy cannot function. Today, in a climate where we are more risk averse in many areas of our lives, Paglia's argument is a call to arms for both men and women to take risks in their intimate lives, as an

---

[26] Everything's Awesome and Camille Paglia Is Unhappy!, *Reason*, 19 March 2015 http://goo.gl/sLTf1J

assertion of authority and judgement against the forces of external regulation and control.

Of course, Paglia acknowledges that women shoulder a greater burden of risk than men. They are far more likely to be victims of rape than men. Brownmiller was at least partly right when she pointed out that the biological make-ups of men and women inevitably create a kind of power imbalance, which cannot be corrected simply by appeal to women being stronger or more assertive. But today, the future of intimate life depends upon women's willingness to take these risks. The more we accept the management and interference of our close personal interactions in the name of avoiding the risks inherent in such interaction, the more we close down the possibility for genuine intimacy.

Rape culture and young people

The appalling impact of the rape culture argument on freedom, on our humanity and on our justice system — which we will discuss in the next chapter — makes it all the more tragic that the key demographic for the argument is among the young. Up and down the country, a new generation of young people are being encouraged to think of one another as potential rapists. As we have seen, many of the movements which arise against different instances of 'rape culture' emanate from university campuses. This has led some commentators to believe that the persistence of the rape culture argument can be blamed on the appointment of feminist professors who keep the rape culture argument alive through their students. But this ignores the fact that the sense of vulnerability and isolation which is encouraged through the rape culture argument is often found to be evident in other areas of young people's lives today. The rape culture argument is accordingly one that fits with the outlook of a section of contemporary young people, irrespective of who happens to be teaching it to them.

The appeal of the rape culture argument among the young makes sense, considering the problematisation of intimacy by the adults around them. We saw earlier how modern PSHE lessons are filled with warnings about the abuse that can permeate close relationships. In 2013, the coalition government amended its definition of domestic violence to include those relationships between the ages of sixteen and eighteen. The focus of the redefinition was the inclusion of 'emotional harm', which could be inflicted by overbearing behaviour and persistent contact. If you search online for the phrase 'young people intimate relationships', the first result is a recent report by the NSPCC into partner exploitation and violence in teenage intimate relationships. The next twenty entries list similar reports by a number of charities, all of which seek to 'expose' the extent of violence and partner 'control' in teenage relationships. The problematisation of intimacy among the young is not restricted to their romantic relationships. In 2014, it was reported that many primary schools were taking the government's stand a step further by introducing 'no best friend' polices, in order to avoid the emotional hurt of having to break such friendships up. Apparently, for today's young people, it is better to have never loved at all rather than to have loved and lost.

When intimacy is problematised so readily among the young, it is hardly surprising that they are also often found to be lonely. Research published by the University of Bolton in 2015 found that more than a quarter of respondents interact socially with others only once a week. Experiences of loneliness were most common in those aged between eighteen and thirty-four, which is all the more disturbing given that this was until recently such a socially active period in people's lives.[27]

These concerns about intimacy are also reflected in the panic around 'sexting'. In 2014, the NSPCC released a report suggesting that young people were regularly sending explicit pictures of themselves to each other. They found that sexting was becoming rapidly more popular, with a significant increase

---

[27]   Bolton psychologist puts loneliness research on the menu, University of Bolton, 17 April 2015 http://goo.gl/bCiIyf

4. *The Impact of Rape Panic*

in calls to Childline by young people referring to the phenomenon.[28] While the evidence around 'sexting' is arguably flawed, and those involved in the issue are prone to exaggerating the extent of the problem, any emerging trend which does exist around sexting is understandable when young people are so often told that real, private relationships are so risky. If young people are sending pictures of themselves to one another more regularly than they once did, perhaps this reflects the fact that keeping relationships private, that engaging in unmonitored intimate relationships, is constantly portrayed to young people as potentially dangerous. Given the extent that campaign groups and teachers emphasise the dangers of intimate relationships, it would hardly be surprising if sending a rude picture of yourself to a boyfriend or girlfriend has taken the place of old forms of youthful intimate behaviour.

The problematisation of intimacy in the adult world is manifested in trends among young people towards self-concern. In the lead-up to the 2015 general election, a poll carried out for The Conversation UK showed that young people were overwhelmingly more concerned with political issues that related to themselves. For example, eighteen percent of young people said tuition fees was the single most important issue in the election. This was followed by 'job prospects for young people', mentioned by twelve percent of respondents. In contrast, healthcare and foreign affairs were cited by only two percent of respondents as the most important issues. The fact that the issues chosen by young people as most important were those directly related to their individual interests suggests a generational prioritising of personal well-being over other social and political concerns.

This tendency towards self-concern is reflected in the fact that student politics is often focused around regulations to avoid any risks of harm to student self-esteem. Today's university campuses are a hotbed of regulation around what

---

[28]   Sexting: advice for parents, NSPCC http://goo.gl/Vo8ziz

can and cannot be said. The online magazine *Spiked*, where I am legal editor, recently undertook a survey of policies at UK universities to reveal which ones undermine freedom of speech. The results showed that eighty percent of universities in the UK had restricted or actively censored free speech through the adoption of various safe space and anti-bullying policies.[29] A review of recent decisions by individual university students' unions shows a contemporary obsession with acknowledging individual identity groups, and protecting individual notions of identity at the expense of free expression. Absurdly, this trend recently culminated in a NUS Women's Conference meeting passing a motion that 'gay men should stop appropriating black women', following allegations that too many homosexual men had been doing impersonations of black women in their communications with one another. This obsession with individual identity over and above all other concerns speaks to a deep cultural narcissism within student politics, whereby any meaningful political agenda becomes held hostage to the needs of individual identity groups.

Once they leave campus, the self-orientation of contemporary millennials is reflected in a profound fear of growing older. All generations arguably fear ageing in some capacity, but few previously have appeared so reluctant to even begin to enter adulthood than the millennials. Numerous articles point to the fact that many young adults have an 'extended adolescence' lasting into their late twenties.[30] Many millennials will blame this on economic factors, which they say prevent them buying a house or even moving away from their parents. But this ignores the fact that young people today are reluctant to commit to anything. The next generation of retirees are expected to have changed jobs eleven times in the course of their lives. Rates of cohabitation, in preference to marriage, are

---

29   Free Speech University Rankings, *Spiked* http://goo.gl/ZzGTbt
30   See, for example, 'Why Millennials Can't Grow Up', *Slate*, 2 December 2013 http://goo.gl/pjeN3O

rising year on year. The age that people get married is similarly increasing, as is the age that people have children. This aversion to commitment of any kind, an elevation of temporary satisfaction and self-validation over and above traditional commitments, shows that today's young people are fundamentally sceptical about committing to anything that carries the potential to impact on their self-esteem.

It is arguably here, among young people, that the rape culture argument stands to do most harm. Today, young people are inundated with information about their own vulnerability — particularly in the context of their intimate relationships. Accordingly, they demonstrate an inclination towards isolation and narcissism. The rape culture argument seeks to cultivate that same sense of vulnerability in the most private area of young people's lives. It destroys any possibility for the development of independent judgement about their relationships. It compels them to become reliant on a whole host of experts to tell them how to live with one another. Students' union officers, the police, PSHE teachers and psychotherapists become the arbiters of their private lives. While the generation before them shook off the social constraints around intimacy, abandoning the old ways of living intimate life and embracing freedom and non-judgmentalism, we are now saddling young people with endless new bureaucratic standards by which they should live intimately with one another, holding their behaviour up to judgement by standards that have nothing to do with genuine, real-life, human intimacy.

Conclusion

The heart of the rape culture argument is an encouragement to see oneself as inherently vulnerable. While in the 1970s and '80s, women did face genuine social barriers to having rape acknowledged and dealt with, today those social barriers are imagined by the rape culture proponents to be evident in everything, from raunchy pop songs to immature 'laddish' behaviour. Today, rape culture is merely a means of expressing a sense of vulnerability with the world. It has little to do with the reality of rape.

Of course, this is potentially devastating for our intimate lives. If we continue to see one another as inherently threatening then it is difficult to see how the kind of trust required for genuine intimacy can develop. But the rape culture argument also impacts on our ability to deal with actual allegations of rape in the real world. It encourages its adherents to abandon the normal systems of justice which have, as we have seen, become far more forceful in their prosecution of rape. The argument that we live in a rape culture has given rise to its own form of justice, one in which truth is sacrificed at the altar of self-validation and emotional payoff.

Five

Hashtag Justice
The Courts of Social Media

One of the central themes of the argument around rape culture is that the justice system is ill-equipped to deal with allegations of rape and sexual violence. Having worked in the UK justice system, I am not naive to the fact that in this regard, they have a point. However, the impact of this argument has not helped the problems that persist in the justice system. In recent years, the argument that we live in a rape culture has contributed to a departure from due process in both the US and the UK. This has been evident both at the level of official investigations and more so in the increasingly informal treatment of allegations. Social media have figured significantly in the move away from due process. Today, it is becoming more and more common to use social and other online media to disseminate an allegation as widely as possible, in order to cause an impact—often involving some degree of punishment to the accused—while avoiding the need to have the allegation tested objectively. We will see that these allegations, which often involve disclosing extremely intimate details about an individual's sex life, are now considered to be matter of public titillation, offered up by those directly involved. Often this is justified on the basis that it allows complainants to have a 'voice' that they are denied by the failing justice system.

Today, the move away from due process around rape and sexual violence takes on two forms. Firstly, the establishment of informal, often online, tribunals to pursue allegations without the need to engage in the objectivity of the justice system. But secondly, the departure from normal procedures within the justice system itself. These two forms of the departure from due process share a common goal: providing affirmation and validation to the experiences of complainants without subjecting their allegations to any objective scrutiny. What these tribunals provide is not justice, nor the truth. They are only capable of providing a very weak form of therapy, or some idea of closure to those making complaints. The kind of closure offered by these new forms of justice is likely to be fleeting, because in bypassing the normal forums for establishing the truth with impartiality, the closure offered necessarily rings hollow.

But worse, the criminal courts — or the online courts — can never provide the kind of intimate help that people who are worried about their intimate experiences require. Through looking at these new tribunals, I have been shocked at how purportedly vulnerable people, those who think of themselves as having been victims of sex crime, feel that the only way of coping with the incident is to open it up to the most public judgement possible. The examples that follow should not just be seen as an indictment on the argument that we live in a rape culture. They are a sad indication of the state of our contemporary discussion around intimacy. The very existence of the tribunals in this chapter is not evidence that we are more capable of offering those who suffer problems with their intimate lives the kind of support they deserve. It merely demonstrates that we, as a society, lack the resources to cope adequately when intimate life presents serious problems.

Victims and complainants — setting the scene for hashtag justice

The new courts of social media do not arise in a vacuum. Rather, they have as their precedent the move away from the objective search for truth that has been a feature of many high-profile investigations by the British state around sexual allegations. We have seen this reflected in earlier chapters, in the causal spread of misinformation around rape from those who are charged with dealing with it, the police and prosecutorial authorities. However, the move away from objectivity is not just evident in the state's treatment of information, but also in their treatment of allegations themselves. Since the commencement of Operation Yewtree, the prosecuting authorities in Britain have relegated the search for truth in many high-profile cases to a secondary concern, in favour of publicly affirming and validating the experience of those making allegations. This has been evident recently in two high profile cases of alleged child sexual abuse, one involving Jimmy Saville and the other involving Labour peer Greville Janner.

Many commentators point out that Operation Yewtree represented a renewed focus on behalf of prosecuting authorities on sexual crime. What is less often pointed out is that, from the beginning of Operation Yewtree, the normal rules of investigating and due process were partially suspended, in order to achieve a result that appeared to honour and confirm the experience of the complainants. When the police published their report into Jimmy Savile in 2013, it was called *Giving Victims a Voice*.[1] The report marked the culmination of a lengthy and costly examination of the allegations surrounding the television presenter. The report acknowledged that because Savile was dead, none of the allegations could be tested in the normal way. Instead, the complainants' allegations would be treated as 'proven' evidence. This meant that the report would not refer to those making allegations as 'complainants', as would be normal in a criminal case until a conviction had been obtained, but rather as 'victims'. The change in language signified that the word of the complainants was going to be treated as true, notwithstanding the fact that their claims could not be tested in the normal way.

---

[1]   David Gray and Peter Watt, *Giving Victims a Voice: Joint report into sexual allegations made against Jimmy Savile*, MPS and NSPCC, January 2013 http://goo.gl/RfM0vb

Today, the distinction between the words 'victim' and 'complainant' is often elided by prosecutors when discussing sex cases.[2] This is significant. In recent history, the distinction between the two concepts represented the importance of the presumption of innocence in the criminal justice system. Accounts were not simply taken to be true, rather they were treated as allegations until they were proven to be true in front of a jury or suitable tribunal. Today, that distinction is often ignored by the police and prosecutors. This demonstrates that the perceived failures of the past are propelling our prosecuting authorities to move away from their traditional role in society, as objective and impartial operators of the justice system. Instead, they now offer an official form of therapy, through blindly acknowledging the status of complainants as victims without testing their allegations fairly. As we saw in an earlier chapter, the outcome of this is not a better treatment of complainants at the hands of a justice system. In fact, it detracts from the state's ability to offer justice, the one form of 'closure' it is uniquely able to offer over and above the less official avenues of support available to the complainants in these cases.

This shift in language has acted as a precedent for other high-profile investigations into sexual violence. In 2015, there were calls for the Labour peer and former MP Lord Janner to face prosecution even though he had been diagnosed with severe dementia. Janner has been accused of twenty-two counts of sexual assault against boys between 1969 and 1988. When the Crown Prosecution Service announced that it would not seek to prosecute Janner in light of the diagnosis, there were calls for him to face scrutiny by a public inquiry. The justification for calling on an octogenarian to face questioning about an allegation he had no hope of understanding and which had occurred decades ago, was that the complainants 'had a right to

---

2   For example, today's CPS policy documents consistently refer to individuals
     in the stage of making an allegation as 'victims'. See 'Rape and Sexual
     Offences: Chapter 5: Victims and Witnesses', CPS http://goo.gl/tGZoUj

have their voices heard'. In other words, it did not matter that Janner could not assist the court in establishing the truth. What mattered was that the complainants—often referred to as 'victims'—would have their experiences confirmed by an official tribunal.

In April 2015, the Goddard Inquiry into child sex abuse announced it would investigate the 'factual basis of the allegations' against Janner, notwithstanding the fact that Janner would not be in a position to defend himself. As this book was being completed, it was reported that the original CPS decision not to prosecute Janner had been overturned through the CPS's process of victim's review. Janner would face a criminal court after all, in the form of a 'trial of the facts'. The reliance on this procedure in a case where the defendant posed no threat to society whatsoever was unprecedented and showed the emphasis that the modern prosecutorial system places on offering therapeutic closure, over and above its traditional role in offering objectively established justice.[3]

We will see that the British state's abandonment of truth and objectivity in its investigation of sexual violence is mirrored in the way that rape and sexual violence are treated by sections of the public in both the UK and the US. The following are just some of the now numerous instances in which the informal, mostly online tribunals have intervened to bestow validation on a particular allegation, often at the expense of any hope of establishing the truth. Welcome to the world of hashtag justice.

Uncle Terry: fashion's famous 'pervert'

Terry Richardson is arguably the most successful fashion photographer of recent years. He has worked with the world's biggest stars in music and film. For a decade, he has been lauded by the fashion world for creating challenging and

---

[3]   CPS decision not to prosecute Lord Janner 'to be overturned', *Guardian*, 26 June 2015 http://goo.gl/ZprpJC

distinctive portraiture photography. He has also spent his career taking 'risqué' shots of models about a third of his age. Much of his work includes sexually explicit material. If I were being more direct, I would say that Richardson is partly known for making respectable porn. His book, *Terryworld*, which was published in 2004, includes photos of models performing sex acts on him as well as numerous photographs of himself posing in the nude.

In early 2014, an anonymous story was posted on the website Reddit. The author was a young woman who claimed to have modelled for Richardson when she was nineteen. The girl indicates that she had modelled nude for other photographers in the past and had been 'comfortable' and even 'empowered' by the experience. She details how she attended Richardson's apartment having submitted her photograph to him. She explains that Richardson's female assistant made her feel comfortable while Richardson prepared to shoot her. In an interview for *Vocativ* a week later, the author—now named as Charlotte Waters—explained what happened:

'He put his thumb in my mouth, which I also thought was weird, but I just let it go. And then he backed off and asked me to start undressing. I went in knowing I was going to have to do that, so at this point I'm still totally comfortable. He was having me take stuff off in stages and taking photos all along the way. He and his assistant were both complimenting a lot, which was a little different from what I had experienced before... So eventually all my clothes were off, and he's still taking pictures. Then he comes over and asks me to hold the top of his jeans while he takes pictures pointing down. At this moment, things were starting to go in a direction that wasn't good, but for some reason, I still had a lot of trust in whatever he told me to do, so I just did it. But then he had me unbutton his pants, and he took his penis out, and it was all completely downhill from there.'[4]

Vocativ had, the previous week, published an article on Richardson called 'The Terry Richardson timeline of skeez'.[5] The article detailed a series of allegations which have been made against Richardson throughout his career. The article did not hold back in its accusatory tone. It called Richardson a 'shameless pervert' and an 'alleged sexual predator', even though no formal allegation has never been made against him.

The articles led to a Twitter-based campaign called '#nomoreterry', which sought to shame any publication that published Richardson's work. Tweeters were encouraged to cancel their subscriptions to big-name American magazines, like *Harper's Bazaar* and *Vogue*, on the basis that they continued to work with Richardson. By the end of April 2014, *Vogue* had indicated that it would never print Richardson's work again. When *Rolling Stone* magazine used Richardson's work, it was used as an example of the prevalent rape culture within photography. When the actor Alan Cumming posted a picture of himself with Richardson after a shoot for *Harper's Bazaar*, the level of Twitter hatred levelled at him made him delete the tweet and publicly apologise for associating himself with Richardson.

More and more allegations began to emerge. In one case, an ex-model sent a lengthy email to the website *Jezebel*, which then published the entire email in full. It detailed how Richardson and his 'now infamous' assistant had been hired to take photographs at a party. Richardson had invited the model back to his apartment for an 'impromptu shoot'. The email went on:

> Then he entered the shot and Leslie snapped a few of us together. He had me kind of crouch down on the floor as I

---

4   'Oh My God, What's Happening?' Up Close and Personal With a Terry Richardson Model, *Vocativ*, 11 March 2014 http://goo.gl/dbLR7o

5   The Terry Richardson timeline of skeez, *Vocativ*, 5 March 2014 http://goo.gl/OqcFYq

moved around, posing. Then, suddenly, I felt a dick pressing into the side of my face. Terry Richardson's semi-hard penis was plunged into the outside of my cheek, and he was jabbing it into my face. Leslie giggled, and muttered something to the effect of, 'Isn't this fun?!' He pressed it to my lips. He clearly wanted a blow job and wanted it documented on camera. I didn't want to act scared or angry because I was in this guy's apartment with no one else around aside from his equally screwed-up assistant and who knows what these psychos were capable of, so I merely muttered something about having to get back to the party and jetted the hell out of there.[6]

At the end of the email, the magazine invited anyone who had 'had an encounter with Uncle Terry and his dick' to get in contact.

Today, the fashion world is effectively split over how Richardson should be treated. One profile of him summed up the divide: 'Richardson: artist or predator?' Everyone has to take a side on Richardson's case. Richardson is one of the first defendants in the new courtrooms of hashtag justice. Everyone in the world is a member of the informal, rabbling jury. No one has ever made a formal complaint against Richardson in relation to sexual assault. Instead, the internet has been used to jump straight to punishing him. He has, effectively, been lynched by an online Twitter mob, which has used the untested, ambiguous historical allegations of Richardson's models to attempt to destroy his career and his body of work.

Richardson's online trial was particularly bizarre, considering the nature of his work, for which he had been lauded for over a decade. The campaign has effectively invited the complete reinterpretation of his work from 'risqué' and 'boundary pushing' to a documented history of sexual violence. Responding to the allegations, Richardson wrote in an article for the *Huffington Post*:

---

6   'I felt a dick pressing into my face': Terry Richardson strikes again, *Jezebel*, 11 June 2014 http://goo.gl/dW4OLT

'Like Robert Mapplethorpe, Helmut Newton, and so many others before me, sexual imagery has always been a part of my photography. Ten years ago, in 2004, I presented some of this work at a gallery show in New York City, accompanied by a book of the photos. The show was very popular and highly praised. The images depicted sexual situations and explored the beauty, rawness and humor that sexuality entails. I collaborated with consenting adult women who were fully aware of the nature of the work, and as is typical with any project, everyone signed releases.'[7]

Even if you take every word of the complaints against Richardson to be true, it is not clear that any crime has taken place. Richardson sounds like a creep, but it is never clear whether he ever knew about his model's discomfort with what he was doing. In Waters's story, the line between her consent and his pressure is blurred. What happens in front of Richardson's camera is inevitably a difficult power play, in which Richardson pushes the boundaries of what his models will do for the sake of what he considers to be art. Of course, commentators are right when they say that the balance of power was weighted towards Richardson. But can the models honestly say they were surprised? All of his models knew the nature of Richardson's work. Undoubtedly, some of these women felt violated. But an important element in assessing Richardson's culpability is assessing what these models knew about what Richardson was thinking when he shot them.

The retroactive reinterpretation of these photo-shoots speaks to the current challenge to intimate judgement. Events which are 'creepy', ambiguous and uncomfortable — and I imagine shooting with Richardson ticks all those boxes — become reinterpreted as sexual violence. If these models felt as though they had been sexually assaulted by Richardson, then they are entitled to have their complaint listened to, investigat-

---

[7]   Correcting the rumors, *Huffington Post*, 14 March 2014
      http://goo.gl/2jTAoS

ed and acted upon. But hashtag justice does none of these things. It merely presents an account of a particular event to the world, and invites unquestioning confirmation of its status as an incident of sexual violence.

The hashtag-justice movement has targeted a number of high-profile individuals in recent years. The Canadian radio presenter Jian Ghomeshi was the target of an investigation by a newspaper, supported by a Twitter campaign, that led to his arrest for sexual assault. Following the public accusations against Ghomeshi, a Twitter hashtag, '#beenrapedneverreported', began trending in which women shared stories about their rape and sexual violation that had not been reported to the police. Women across the world began sharing their stories of sexual violation with social media, in an apparent attempt to 'set the shame (of being raped) free'. US comedian Bill Cosby, who has recently been publicly accused of rape and sexual assault, has faced a targeted campaign to boycott his shows. None of the above have yet been convicted of any criminal action.

But these new forms of tribunal are not only imposed on the great and the good. They also target lesser-known public figures who, by attracting a particular following, leave themselves open to the campaigns of hashtag justice.

The Casualties

The Casualties are an American punk rock band. They formed in the 1990s in New York, and have attracted a decent following. On 5 November 2013, a guest contributor called 'Elizabeth' posted a comment on a parenting blog. It made an allegation of sexual assault against the lead singer of the band, Jorge Herrera. The blogger conceded that she could not remember any of the details regarding the allegation. She could not remember where the assault had happened or when. But she did remember approaching fans of the band and telling her story. She said:

> The one amazing thing all of these complete strangers had in common was that they BELIEVED ME. They felt compelled to

talk, cry, relate, or brainstorm. Like this was a totally fucked up thing that happened and we were not gonna sit by and take it anymore. In the end, 100% of the people I talked to removed the shirt/patch/pin/etc of the band. One boy even took his shirt off and heaved it into a fire. All really small gestures to you, but to me it felt really empowering to tell my story. To have someone, through actions, say, 'Yeah man. I'm on YOUR side.' 'You can only be a victim if you admit defeat', were words I lived by.'[8]

The blog gave a very short description of what she was alleging:

This man cornered me in a room and tried to force me to perform sexual acts on him, stating he would tell everyone in the van I did it anyway so I might as well. When I fled the room, he chased me down the hall, pinning me against a wall and shoving his hands down every orifice he could find while shoving his mouth over mine to prevent my muffled screams and tears from being heard.

As the author only gave her first name, it is impossible to identify her. The site's editor later insisted that 'at least two people' working for the website knew the blogger personally. She had not been to the police and did not intend to. When another journalist contacted the blogger through the website, she declined to be interviewed, indicating that she was happy that the blog had become a safe space for people to discuss the allegations against the singer. The comments section on the site was inundated with stories of sexual assault and molestation, some involving Herrera, some not.

On 28 November, a further blog was published titled 'a partial list of accounts about Jorge from The Casualties'. The blogger had established an email address specifically to receive stories of sexual assault perpetrated by Herrera.

---

8   Guest post: I won't apologise for being assaulted, *Put Your Damn Pants On*, 5 November 2013 http://goo.gl/UOAuTp

Much like Richardson, the punk world became split on how to respond to the allegations against The Casualties. Two rival Facebook pages were set up, one arguing that The Casualties' gigs should be boycotted, the others arguing that the boycott itself was absurd. Protests were organised at the band's gigs. When the band played in Denver, a group of protesters blocked the van as it was attempting to move equipment into the venue and a number of protesters were arrested.

The band eventually published a response to the allegations. They bemoaned the lack of due process afforded to Herrera, and the impact that the allegations had had on their lives:

> The accused has to prove his innocence and when witnesses step forth to do just that, they are being ignored. Rumours are spread, copied, repeated and not a single thought of the human person they target wasted. In all those months since these lies and slander started, nothing has been published that would prove Jorge's guilt. No evidence. No witnesses. No court case. Nothing.[9]

The Casualties learned a lesson about the world of hashtag justice. In order to enact punishment, these informal online tribunals don't need evidence, because the point is not to find out the truth. Hashtag justice is merely a forum through which individual experience is validated and confirmed in the most public way possible. It is a peculiar form of contemporary show trial, in which the most intimate aspects of people's lives are thrown into the public realm for scrutiny and judgement. It is a truly odd world, in which the 'shame and stigma' of being the victim of sexual assault is combated by broadcasting detailed allegations across social media.

Of course, when we are talking about celebrities, we might think that hashtag justice is merely part of a broader celebrity

---

9   The Casualties release statement on sexual assault allegations against frontman, *Dying Scene*, 8 February 2014 http://goo.gl/ZkoGxQ

culture of gossip. But the real-world impact of hashtag justice struck me with force in early 2015, when I realised that the same methods which had been used to vilify those who had placed themselves in the public eye, the likes of Richardson and Cosby, could be used to target pretty much anyone who had any sort of following on which they depended.

In early 2015, a short-lived campaign centred on Cambridge University saw hashtag justice turn against a small kebab shop, The Gardenia – usually known locally as Gardies - which had been selling kebabs to the students of one of the world's most elite universities for the past twenty-five years. In mid-March, an anonymous blogpost was published claiming that the author had been sexually assaulted by a member of staff at the cafe. In the post, it was claimed that she had gone to the cafe drunk, bought food and sat to eat it in the upstairs area. A member of staff had sat with her, but when she had tried to leave he had got in her way and refused to move until she kissed him. When she tried to move past him he had taken it as an 'invitation to put his hands on me'.

A campaign was launched for Cambridge students to boy-cott the cafe. Given that a significant amount of the cafe's revenue came from the student population, this was not an idle threat. A Facebook page was set up explaining:

> Gardies are aware that a member of their staff is behaving in an unacceptable way to drunk women. This has gone on for years, and everyone 'has a story', and it's so overt that they cannot have missed it. No matter what they say, no matter what statement of incredulity they put out, we know that they know who this is aimed at. We don't know his name. We barely know what he looks like and frankly, it doesn't matter. This is not a kangaroo court—but the evidence is mounting: and they need to deal with it.

Of course, their defensiveness was apposite. A kangaroo court is exactly what the campaign turned into. The page stated a series of 'demands', which included reviewing all the CCTV held by the restaurant for evidence of the attacks and immedi-ately firing the person responsible. The owner of the cafe, who had owned and run Gardies for twenty-five years, explained that he was unaware of any allegations of sexual assault against his staff. He had to be informed about the campaign by two Iranian students, who happened to know him personally. He was taken aback by the allegations, not least because no one from the Boycott Gardies campaign had told him about the allegations. They had not given him the opportunity to investigate or take action. Instead, they had immediately set up a Facebook page.

The campaign put the owner in an impossible position. The group were unable to provide the times or dates of any of the allegations, meaning that he would have to review hundreds of hours of CCTV. The students assisting him effectively had to translate for him and act as intermediaries between him and the students. They told me:

> It was very difficult for (the owner of Gardies). Because he does not know the dates of any assaults he is unable to check the CCTV footage. He does not have the time to check all the videos from the last month to track down the incident. Plus he does not speak very good English, so much of what the campaign is asking for we have to translate. He is very worried about the campaign and the impact on his business. At the end of the day he just wants to feed his family.

Bizarrely, the students targeting Gardies saw little moral ambiguity about the campaign. The page received in excess of 1,300 'likes' within forty-eight hours. The idea that a man's business, one which had served university students for twenty-five years, should be the subject of a student-led boycott to force it to cave into their utterly unreasonable 'demands' was viewed by most of the users of the Facebook page as a normal outcome for an allegation involving sexual assault.

After two days, threatened with the loss of his livelihood, the owner issued a statement caving in to the student's demands. It was not clear whether the police had become involved, but his statements suggested that he had suspended the member of staff that the allegation related to. Sounding like a truly triumphant and smug lynch mob, the students published a statement on the Facebook page indicating that the boycott had been called off. They said they were 'satisfied and wholly encouraged' by the response from Gardies. In an article for a student newspaper, the *Tab*, one writer celebrated the success of the campaign, suggesting that she too knew people who had 'suffered' sexual assault at the cafe, including one friend who had been the subject of an attempted kiss by one of the waiters.

The Gardies cases, much like that involving the Casualties, illustrates that the lynch-mob model behind hashtag justice can target anyone who depends on a particular group for support. Individuals can effectively be held hostage by pending allegations and forced to cave into 'demands', while having their reputation permanently tarnished by the fact of the allegations themselves. This web-based 'ransoming' is disastrous for any genuine victims of sexual violence. It scuppers the possibility for any objective investigation and makes it extremely difficult for any proper adjudication of the case to happen. At the same time, it holds ordinary people up to an online show-trial, which denies them the right to impartial and fair treatment.

It was not students who set up the template for the weird world of hashtag justice, but the authorities. It was the report into Savile and others, published at the outset of Operation Yewtree, which openly accepted that its purpose was not to get at the truth but to give 'voice' to those making allegations against Savile. The courts of hashtag justice are mirror images of the bizarre public show trials that are happening at the highest levels of the British establishment, which—much like the fevered campaigns spilling out across social media—prioritise the validation of individual experience over the objective establishment of truth.

The presumption of innocence

Perhaps the most significant safeguard on state power is the presumption of innocence. Yet, what these cases consistently suggest is that in the world of hashtag justice, the presumption of innocence simply does not apply. In fact, the very issue of innocence is thrown in question. For many of those who believe that we live in a rape culture, allegations are automatically assumed to be true—supported by data suggesting the low prevalence of false rape claims—and official findings of innocence merely provide further evidence that the 'rape culture' has prevented the truth from being found. When you believe in a rape culture you don't believe in innocence, you merely believe in those rapists who have been caught and those who have 'gotten away with it' because of the endemic influence of toxic cultural misogyny.

This was shown in stark detail in May 2014, when the president of the Oxford Union, Ben Sullivan, was arrested for rape and attempted rape. Sullivan was twenty-one at the time of his arrest. It was reported that he was a member of a notorious student society at Oxford, known as the 'Banter Squadron'. The squadron were allegedly a debauched drinking society and were apparently notorious for their exploits with women students. For many, Sullivan's arrest confirmed what they already knew about the 'squadron': that they were entitled posh boys who couldn't keep it in their trousers long enough.[10]

Following his arrest, Sullivan was bailed. While on bail, he decided to retain his place as the chair of the Oxford Union. He had not been charged with any offence nor was there any suggestion of any evidence against him beyond the word of those complaining. He was, in the eyes of the law and society, an entirely innocent man until proven otherwise.

But in the world of hashtag justice, this hardly mattered. Almost immediately, the case in the court of hashtag justice had effectively concluded and his punishment began to be processed. An online open letter was written by Oxford University Student Union's vice president for women, Sarah

---

[10]   Dragged from bed at dawn, branded a rapist, his reputation trashed: President of Oxford Union tells the utterly horrific story of his year-long nightmare, *Daily Mail*, 21 June 2014 http://goo.gl/MsOt6c

Pine, calling on Sullivan to resign. Students began contacting speakers who had been booked at the Union to inform them of Sullivan's arrest and to invite them to withdraw their attendance. Bizarrely, the letters calling for them to withdraw their attendance described the move as a 'push for equality'.

Some speakers obliged. In a truly surreal series of statements it seemed that, all of a sudden, the chairmanship of the Oxford Union became a matter of national public concern. The open letter penned by the SU was published by the *New Statesman*, a leading current-affairs magazine. The head of Interpol issued a statement about the case, justifying his decision to withdraw from speaking at the Union:

> What should the head of a society like the Oxford Union do if he is under investigation for rape and attempted rape? In my view, he should be guided by the best interests of his organisation. He should not be guided by his own interests. In this case my advice to Ben Sullivan would be either to resign or take a leave of absence until the criminal investigation has been completed.[11]

In the utterly peculiar world of hashtag justice, the head of an international police agency can think it appropriate to comment on student politics and to compel a young man to give up his position at a student society. More and more celebs came out against Sullivan, calling on him to step down in the name of 'equality'. Only one, philosopher AC Grayling, raised the issue of Sullivan's possible innocence and refused to withdraw his commitment, writing in a letter to Sarah Pine:

> Asking people to convict and punish someone before due process of law has taken its course is a bad direction to go in and with great respect I urge you to reflect on that.

---

[11] Oxford Union boycott after president returns despite police investigation, *Telegraph*, 21 May 2014 http://goo.gl/gBw6YC

Notwithstanding the awkward issue of Sullivan's possible innocence, the process of his online prosecution continued. An article in June claimed that Sullivan's case showed the extent to which society engages in victim blaming on an 'endemic' level. Pine, the author of the open letter to Sullivan, penned an article following his clearance. She said the case, rather than showing the dangers inherent in running blind with unproven allegations, showed how Oxford showed symptoms of 'rape culture'. In the article, she consistently refers to the complainant against Sullivan as a 'survivor', showing that she had already concluded the truth of the allegation notwithstanding the lack of any prosecution. She wrote:

> Sullivan's case has also demonstrated the way that people will actively seek to disregard survivors' experiences of rape. Sullivan was president of Oxford's debating club, the Oxford Union. Sullivan's presidency was untenable and offensive after his arrest. Whilst he has now not been charged, at the time the potential for charge was worrying. Generally when people are arrested for rape, they step down from their positions as a mark of respect for survivors of these very serious crimes. To do otherwise sends a message that when people report, it will not be taken seriously. However, he did not step down.

The problem with Pine's position is that the allegations appear to be false. After Sullivan was told he would not be charged, further evidence emerged suggesting that he may have been the subject of a malicious accusation. The *Daily Mail* interviewed Sullivan after it was announced that the charges against him had been dropped. The interview suggested that messages had been received by Sullivan from the complainant indicating that her friends had 'misinterpreted' her tears on the night of the alleged assault and that she had not meant it to go as far as it did.

Of course, in hindsight, it would have been better for everyone if the allegations had been dealt with discreetly. Instead, the court of hashtag justice thrust these allegations into the public gaze, to be played out like episodes of *Hollyoaks*, complete with celebrity cameos. The desperate rush to judgement is an insult to the severity of what is being alleged. While those who argue that we live in a 'rape culture' suggest that a bigoted and misogynistic society makes dealing with the reality of rape far harder, they ignore the fact that the incessant drive to publicise rape allegations, to make them the source of salacious rumour and gossip, does more to undermine the severity of rape in our society than Robin Thicke's 'Blurred Lines' ever could.

YouTube Justice

Today, such is the appeal of hashtag justice that allegations of rape and sexual assault can be uploaded to YouTube and broadcast to the world, without the rest of the world batting an eyelid. In 2014, a series of YouTube stars were accused of sexually assaulting and raping their young fans. The allegations—all made by young women in their teens—were all uploaded as YouTube videos. The stars themselves responded over YouTube videos. Channel 4 News, rather than denouncing the absolutely bizarre tendency for young people to broadcast serious allegations of sex crime over the internet, reported on the cases as if they were playing out in court. For all the official criticism and concern for young people sending each other sexual text messages, or 'sexting', which has led children's charities and the government to go into an overdrive of panic and regulation, there has been no concern at all about young people sharing their stories of sexual abuse, which are lapped up by the media and reported as if the process was a serious criminal investigation.

The most prominent of the cases was that of Sam Pepper. In 2014, Pepper was a YouTube star. For anyone over eighteen, this may seem like an odd concept, but apparently people can now become rich and famous by posting videos of themselves performing pranks on YouTube. Pepper had done just that, and done it very well. He had earned a lot of money and relocated to Los Angeles. His 'pranks' involved handcuffing himself to women and refusing to unlock them until they kissed him as well as lassoing girls in the presence of their boyfriends. His fans were generally accepting of his sexually close-to-the-bone material, presumably choosing to go along with the judgement of those involved in his videos, who tended to be a little creeped out but ultimately charmed and unaffected by Pepper's exploits.

Then, in October 2014, he posted a video to his YouTube account which saw him on the streets of Los Angeles pinching girls' bums with a fake hand he had concealed under his jumper. The video was received badly. Overnight, thousands of video responses were posted calling him a sexual predator. Online 'sex educator and feminist' Loci Green posted a video calling Pepper's video an example of sexual harassment, and penned an open letter to Pepper, which received in excess of 100,000 signatures in the first twenty-four hours of being posted. Pepper went on to post two further videos in response to the outcry. The first was the same prank being performed by a woman on unsuspecting men, then a third in which Pepper described the series of videos as a 'social experiment' designed to raise awareness about sexual assault.

That could have been the end of it. But it wasn't. After the series of videos had been posted, another video came to light which had been posted in September. The video was fifteen minutes long and was posted by an account called 'I'm Anonymous'. It was called 'Sam Pepper: The Real Reveal'. In it, a nineteen-year-old woman accuses Pepper of raping her at his apartment. She gives a lengthy and detailed account delivered in black-and-white video. She describes meeting Pepper while working as a waitress in Los Angeles. They exchanged numbers and he invited her to his apartment. When she arrived at his apartment she said she was surprised to find him alone. She goes on to describe her rape in detail.

The video is extremely disturbing viewing. Of course, it is disturbing to hear a serious allegation of sexual violence. But the video is all the more disturbing for the context in which it arises. There is something extremely strange and unsettling about watching a young girl broadcast her rape allegation to the world. You are hearing something which should be heard by someone close to the girl, preferably someone with a sufficient level of adult judgement to give her guidance and care. Instead, the intimate details of this young girl's life are being broadcast to the entire world, without any limitation on its distribution whatsoever.

Further videos followed, making further allegations against Pepper. One video, posted by another young woman, alleged that Pepper had taken her to the cinema and 'tried to put his hands on me while we kissed'. Another video alleged that Pepper had forced her to give him oral sex before one of his shows. Videos were made on popular YouTube channels calling Pepper 'vile scum' and demanding that he be reported to the police. Eventually, the Los Angeles police did intervene in relation to the first allegation of rape, but found the complainant to be 'uncooperative' so the case was dropped.

The YouTube allegation phenomenon is an understandable outcome of the narrative around rape culture. The current panic turns allegations of serious sexual violence into matters of public gossip and entertainment. This is all done under the rubric of 'raising awareness'. But who would sensibly argue that the intimate private details of a young woman's allegation should be used to 'raise awareness' about anything? Others say that these women should be 'given a voice' — but wouldn't that voice be better expressed to those close to them, who might be able to offer genuine support and advice, rather than broadcasting the allegation for the attention of the whole world?

The more I watched these videos, reaching out anonymously to the whole world, the more I thought that the video said just as much about the adult world's inability to confront difficult questions about intimacy and sex as it did about the sexual exploits of a YouTube prankster. The authors of hashtag justice are not those involved. It was not them who turned sexual violence into a matter of individual validation and identity. It was not them that devalued objectivity in our dealings with these allegations in favour of public displays of condemnation. It is not their fault that they feel that the only appropriate forum for disclosing their most intimate problems is the most public forum available to them. The precedent for these informal tribunals can be found in the state's own investigation of sex crime, who has moved further and further away from prioritising the truth around rape and further towards prioritising the affirmation of individual experience. The very fact that the videos exist show that contemporary society faces serious difficulties with guiding young people through the inherently uncertain world of intimate human interaction. These problems are compounded by the argument that we live in a rape culture.

Conclusion

The owner of a kebab shop in Cambridge, photographer Terry Richardson and prankster Sam Pepper have little in common. But one thing they share is their experience of hashtag justice. In each of their cases, allegations have been aired in the most public way possible, disseminated as widely as possible, and then used as a vehicle to enact punishment on them without the normal recourse to due process. It is not only the accused that suffer, of course. Those who arguably suffer the most are the genuine victims. We apparently live in an age in which victims of sexual assault and rape see social and print media as the most viable way of getting their 'voice' heard.

This is a deeply problematic development. Firstly, it scuppers any possibility of a prosecution by airing the most important evidence in public. Secondly, it encourages the idea that allegations are ends in themselves, and that there is nothing to be gained from having the allegation tested.

The public airing of allegations, in these most sensitive of cases, is a symptom of a society that has become less concerned with truth and objectivity and more concerned with fulfilling the subjective emotional needs of alleged victims. The authors of hashtag justice are not the legions of people who sign up to pass judgement in its kangaroo courts—it's the state, the first to move away from objectivity and due process in its adjudication of sex crime. This is not giving victims a 'voice'—it is denigrating the objectivity and seriousness that are vital to adequately dealing with allegations of sexual violence.

But perhaps even worse than the state's abandonment of objectivity and due process when dealing with these allegations is society's failure to provide young people with the resources to cope with problems in their intimate lives. The recourse to YouTube for guidance and closure shows that these young people are not comfortable discussing the intimate areas of their lives with the adults around them. This is wholly understandable, when that adult world has so readily depicted unregulated private intimate life as something to be afraid of. These informal, web-based tribunals are not just a symptom of a justice system that is moving away from due process, it is also a symptom of a society which is less capable of coping when intimate life appears to go seriously wrong. It is this inability to cope with the uncertainty of intimate life that further propels the current panic around rape and rape culture.

Six

Concluding Remarks

At the opening of this book, I drew attention to a report that had been published as the book was being concluded. Within a week of that report being published there has been a further announcement around rape that illustrated the dangers of our current panic. In June 2015, the Crown Prosecution Service published a report into figures around violence against women and girls. The report revealed that 2,581 people were convicted of rape between 2014 and 2015. The media reported that this was the highest number of people ever convicted in a single year.

Much like its presentation of figures around VAWG, which as we saw earlier were highly questionable, the CPS's treatment of the rape statistics was particularly interesting. What was telling was that the Crown had shifted from focusing on the conviction rate, which it had obsessively focused on in its reporting of previous years, to instead focusing on the total number of people convicted in a given year. In 2014/15, as we saw earlier, the conviction rate for rape actually fell by three percentage points. This means that, of all the cases brought to court, fewer cases ended in conviction than in the previous year. This drop in the conviction rate was the second drop of three percentage points in two years. As of 2015, it now stands at fifty-seven percent, which is the same as it was in 2008. In 2013, the CPS was celebrating increasing this rate from fifty-seven percent in 2008 to an 'all-time high'. Now, the rate has reverted right back to where the CPS started. This means that while rape convictions have risen numerically, they have fallen proportionately. Looked at another way, there have been significantly more acquittals in the past twelve months than in previous years. This means that more innocent people have been prosecuted for rape than ever before. This means the CPS has become worse at prosecuting rape.

This latest report merely emphasises how our current discussion around rape and sexual violence is suffering under the panicked and hysterical climate we find ourselves in. This climate is actively preventing the emergence of a rational, constructive discussion about the proper parameters of the law and the areas of potential improvement in the justice system. The argument that we live in a 'rape culture' is only able to survive because our public discussion on rape is so rife with panic and misinformation. We owe it to everyone who has encountered rape in real life to treat it with the objectivity and level-headedness it deserves. This is actively prevented by the persistence of the myth of rape culture.

This short book has sought to challenge the key claims of the rape culture argument and to present the dangers of believing in them. We began by dislodging many of the common myths that exist about rape culture. The persistence of these myths is having a detrimental effect on people's perceptions of society's ability to cope with rape and sexual violence, while justifying further intervention into people's intimate lives. Recent decades have seen the expansion of the law around rape to cover many new areas of sexual behaviour. The impact of the hysteria around rape has been the shutting down of debate around this expansion and the demonisation of anyone who seeks to question it. The argument that we live in a rape culture encourages a deeply harmful notion of inherent vulnerability, which adds to a worrying problematisation of intimacy in wider society. This is likely to have a significant effect on the young, who are often taught that intimate relationships are potentially dangerous. Lastly, we saw how the rape culture argument is affecting due process, leading to the development of informal forms of justice, in which online mobs and pressure groups have a significant say over the outcome of cases, over and above the formal institutions of the justice system.

This is why the discussion around rape culture is more than a feminist issue. Many commentators have described how the development of a particular brand of feminism has driven the arguments around rape culture. This is, to some extent, true, but to hold this narrow group of feminists responsible is to ignore the more fundamental changes that are taking place in society that allow these arguments to survive. These are changes not confined to feminism, but permeate our social discussions around intimacy. In concluding, I want to address some further examples of the impact of rape culture internationally. I then want to offer some remarks on the nature of the intimate sphere, and why we should seek to argue for its protection in the future.

Rolling Stone

As we have seen, the argument that we live in a rape culture emanates substantially from writers working in the United States. Today, some of the most egregious examples of the impact of the claim we live in a rape culture occur Stateside. To cover all of these examples would require another book. We have made reference to some of these examples in the body of this book, but two further American examples cannot be ignored. Firstly, a recent journalistic incident at *Rolling Stone* magazine. Secondly, the development of Title IX lawsuits on American campuses, which is a further reflection of the abandonment of due process around rape that we mentioned in Chapter 5.

In November 2014, *Rolling Stone* committed what it would later term 'an individual and collective journalistic failing'. The magazine published a story called 'A rape on campus'. The story detailed how an anonymous complainant, known as Jackie, had been the victim of a violent gang rape at a fraternity house at the University of Virginia. The story had been written by a journalist for *Rolling Stone* called Sabrina Erdely. According to the story, members of a frat house had thrown Jackie through a glass table, punched her in the face and subjected her to gang rape. The attack had been organised by a young man at the frat house who Jackie knew, and who worked as a lifeguard at a local swimming pool. The account went into grim detail:

> My eyes were adjusting to the dark. And I said his name and turned around... I heard voices and I started to scream and someone pummelled into me and told me to shut up. And that's when I tripped and fell against the coffee table and it smashed underneath me and this other boy, who was throwing his weight on top of me. Then one of them grabbed my shoulders... One of them put his hand over my mouth and I bit him—and he straight-up punched me in the face... One of them said, 'Grab its motherfucking leg'. As soon as they said it, I knew they were going to rape me.[1]

Following its publication, the article immediately caused sensation. It seemed to illustrate perfectly the epidemic of campus rape and sexual assault which had apparently been 'exposed' by the rape awareness movement some forty years earlier. The online version of the article received 2.7million views. At the University of Virginia (UVA), the *Phi Kappa Psi* frat house, where the rape was alleged to have taken place, was the subject of vandalism. Bricks were thrown through the window and graffiti urging the frat to be disbanded was daubed on the outside walls.

But almost immediately after the piece was published, doubts began to be raised about the truth of Jackie's story. In December, less than a month after the original piece was published, the *Washington Post* published an investigation into Jackie's claims that cast serious doubt over some of the central details in her story. *Phi Kappa Psi* had been working with the local police to assist in the investigation of the case. The police concluded that there had not been an event at the house on the

---

[1] 'A Rape on Campus' – What Went Wrong?, *Rolling Stone,* 5 April 2015 http://goo.gl/Lkhq5m

night of the alleged attack. The friends that Jackie had allegedly reported the assault to denied Jackie's claims that they had discouraged her from going to the police. The lifeguard Jackie described as the ringleader of the attack was not a member of the house, as Jackie had claimed. Erdely herself began to doubt the veracity of the story. When she contacted Jackie a week after publication, she realised that Jackie could not remember the surname of the 'lifeguard', a young man she claimed to live in fear of.

The magazine ordered an independent review of the article. The review found that Erdely had effectively accepted exactly what Jackie had said without undertaking any basic fact checking. There had been a failure to undertake 'basic journalistic practice'. The report said:

> The problem was methodology, compounded by an environment where several journalists with decades of collective experience failed to surface and debate problems about their reporting or to heed the questions they did receive from a fact-checking colleague[2].

In other words, Jackie's account was taken entirely at face value. Its truth was assumed from the outset. The *Rolling Stone* UVA saga is more than just an egregious example of journalistic failure. It was an example of how the reporting of rape can suffer from the same abandonment of reality that we have seen in official reporting in the UK. It is a warning to those in the UK who emphasise the need to 'believe' at all costs. There are certain institutions in society that demand proper scepticism in order to function. This kind of scepticism leads to questioning, reasoning and conclusion based on the impartial assessment of evidence. The *Rolling Stone* fiasco shows that the abandonment of objectivity encouraged by the argument that we live in a rape culture is having an impact in the press, as well as in the criminal justice system.

---

2   Ibid.

Title IX

The suspicion of the traditional principles of justice is also affecting the treatment of official rape allegations in the States. Across America, stories are emerging of colleges dealing with complaints of sexual assault via what is known as a Title IX complaint. Title IX of the Education Amendments 1972 is an American civil-rights law that prohibits sexual discrimination on any college campus that receives federal funding. Students can, today, issue a Title IX complaint detailing how their college has violated this provision, which can involve making an allegation of serious sexual violence. The college is then open to adjudicate and pass a punishment based on its own internal findings.

Title IX is now widely deployed in the US as an alternative to pursuing the normal system of justice. The website End Rape on Campus claims that Title IX is an effective way for a 'survivor' to get justice, especially given that the normal justice system is assumed to be unlikely to deliver a conviction. Across the US, informal campus tribunals are being used to settle allegations of serious criminality. Students have been expelled following the findings of these tribunals, and branded sexual offenders without any recourse to proper due process. Bizarrely, this has given rise to counter claims under Title IX from those accused of these offences, on the basis that they have been discriminated against by reference to their gender.

The growing use of Title IX further illustrates how the panic around rape and rape culture expands the remit of informal tribunals in dealing with serious allegations. Of course, the justice systems in both the UK and the US are flawed. There will always be cases that do not get the resolution they deserve. But the growth of these alternatives does not solve this problem, it compounds it. By providing quick routes to punishment, or by celebrating a particular mode of disposing of a case on the basis that you are more likely to 'get a result', the panic around rape and rape culture detracts from the very objectivity and impartiality that we should be striving for in our treatment of all rape cases. The flaws in the justice system will not be corrected by creating our own, especially when these procedures deny those accused of serious crimes the protections that are a prerequisite to a truly just result.

The discussion around rape culture in the US is arguably heightened when compared to the UK. It is, at least, featuring more often in the mainstream debate around sexual violence. There is, arguably, another book to be written about the germination of the argument across the Atlantic. However, I would argue that the important questions facing both the US and UK may be prompted by the allegation that we live in a rape culture, but have little to do with the form or content of that argument itself. The big questions that we should be asking, and which are prevented from being asked by the prevalence of the rape culture argument, relate to what we truly value about intimate life. This question has proved too involved to be covered in a short book on a particular argument. But if this book allows the debate around rape and rape culture to be situated around a discussion regarding intimacy, then we will have taken a small step towards correcting the climate of misinformation and hysteria that we now face.

Intimacy

A common question I was asked while writing this book was: why? It was not clear to a lot of people why rape would be an issue of concern for a man in his late twenties. Their questioning is understandable. While I had recognised that there were issues around the rape discussion that required further interrogation, it was only through my discussions with the people who inspired this book and those who questioned me about my motivations that I became clear in my own head why the book was important.

The reason was that the survival of the rape culture argument was a symptom of a dearth of honest discussion about the value of intimacy. Intimacy is that part of our private lives which relates to our closest relationships with other human beings. How we think about intimacy captures how we think about our families, our loved ones, our children and anyone else with whom we have a close personal bond. These relationships, each with its own individual dynamics, quirks and power relations, have traditionally been situated outside — to some degree — the realm of politics and public life, in a distinct realm where they are free from the rules and expectations that govern life in the outside world.

In the twentieth century, numerous writers drew attention to the emergence of the intimate sphere as a realm traditionally off limits to external regulation and control. Jürgen Habermas, writing in the early 1960s, describes the intimate sphere as an area of private 'self-cultivation'. It was with the emergence of a newly conscious bourgeois public, one capable of forming opinions and having arguments with one another, that the family home became a place of 'experimenting' with one's subjectivity, in the relatively private forum of our intimate relationships. It is with our private relationships with others that we experiment and take risks in a manner that would be inappropriate with someone with whom we lacked such intimacy. For Habermas, the intimate realm in the nineteenth century emerged as a 'training ground' for public life, part of the process of becoming a responsible, public individual, accountable for our public actions because of the process of self-development we have undertaken within the private sphere.[3]

The connection between intimacy and the development of the attributes for use in public life had been described before. The philosopher Hannah Arendt, writing in the 1950s, described the emergence of the intimate realm in opposition to the mass organisation of society. For Arendt, modernity had led to a breakdown in the distinction between the private and public spheres and their replacement with a new sphere of life called 'the social'. She contrasts modernity with the ancient Greek city state, in which a strong distinction between private and public was 'axiomatic'. A citizen's private life was con-

---

[3]   Jürgen Habermas, *The Structural Transformation of the Public Sphere*

cerned with the necessities of living. It was, accordingly, a 'pre-political phenomenon'. Because man, living in private, was governed by the necessities of living, propelled to act by what he needed in order to survive, he was not truly free. Eating, sleeping and the development of the family were a necessary prerequisite for active engagement in public life and the exercise of meaningful freedom. It was only in public that men could strive towards immortality through the achievement of great deeds. Such deeds were only 'great' in the context of the public realm because it was only in that realm that such deeds could be recognised.[4]

Arendt saw, with the coming of modernity, a breakdown of this distinction and the emergence of the private business of necessity into the public realm. 'Society', for Arendt, was occasioned by the destruction of the public sphere, the area of life that allowed for the possibility of transcendence, and its replacement with a mass organisation of individual private life. The emergence of society, over the course of many centuries, had led to the large scale 'normalisation' of human affairs, the breakdown of the 'axiomatic' distinction between public and private life.

It is in this context that intimacy emerges as a new aspect of the private sphere. The gradual 'normalisation' of society leads men into what Arendt called a 'radical subjectivity'. She writes that

> the modern individual and his endless conflicts, his inability either to be at home in society or live outside it all together...the radical subjectivism of his emotional life was born in this rebellion of the heart.

This conception of intimacy, as man's 'rebellion of the heart' against the gradual 'normalisation' of the society around him, his assertion of difference in the face of creeping mass organisa-

---

4   Hannah Arendt, *The Human Condition*

tion, marks the intimate out as a realm cultivated for the expression of individual human judgement.

The fact that intimacy has been historically connected to individual judgement is why its regulation is often depicted in dystopian literature. In the opening chapters of his dystopian novel, *Brave New World*, Aldous Huxley depicts a world in which traditional forms of unregulated human intimacy have become part of a near-forgotten past. Huxley introduces us to the state-owned embryo factory, in which human beings are bred for particular functions after their birth. The process of reproduction is treated as an instrumental accounting exercise, with human beings effectively farmed for different roles in the society they are about to enter. The managers of the factory remember human intimacy with revulsion, referring to sex as a 'hideous' part of man's history.

Of course, we are not in a brave new world of mass reproduction. But Huxley's novel depicts the authoritarian implications of the state becoming involved in the management—and consequent destruction—of intimate life. His vision is of a world in which the state has taken over the management of intimate life entirely, subjecting it to the same rules and standards that governed wider society. Thereby, man's 'intimate rebellion of the heart' has become subjected to the same rules and regulations that govern the external world around him.

The argument of this book is that the intimate realm, this space for self-cultivation, is being challenged by the imposition of external standards on how we live our intimate lives. The panic around rape and rape culture is a symptom of a society that has become deeply anxious about the notion of unregulated intimacy. This not only betrays a mistrust of one another, but a deep mistrust of our own judgement. Today, we are inundated with laws, guidance, expertise, policy and official government mandates that seek to guide us towards the 'correct' way to engage in our intimate relationships. The depletion of this realm of self-cultivation means we are less confident about making decisions about our private lives today. We are also less capable of coping with challenges involving intimate life. This is a big problem, one whose roots go far beyond the narrow feminist discussion on the claims of rape culture.

We are not in a Brave New World. But the persistence of the myth of rape culture demonstrates the need for an honest debate about our intimate lives. The argument that we live in a rape culture has survived for too long, precisely because it seeks to close down grown-up, honest and rational discussion about intimacy, particularly in the context of the law. When this happens, the climate of misinformation and panic that results creates the conditions for the increased and unchallenged intervention of the state and third parties into the most private areas of our lives. The argument that we live in a rape culture is far bigger than feminism. It is far bigger than the technical, legal debates around how we deal with rape trials in our law courts. The dangerous myth of rape culture seeks to portray us all as incapable of living freely, independently and privately with one another. We owe it to ourselves to disbelieve it.